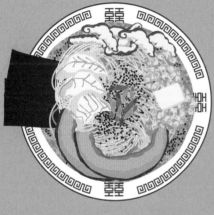

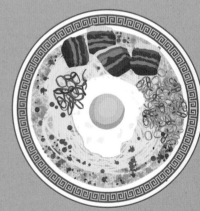

RAMEN-TOPIA

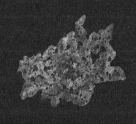

60+ SLURP-TASTIC RECIPES

RAMEN-TOPIA

DEBORAH KALOPER

Smith
Street
Books

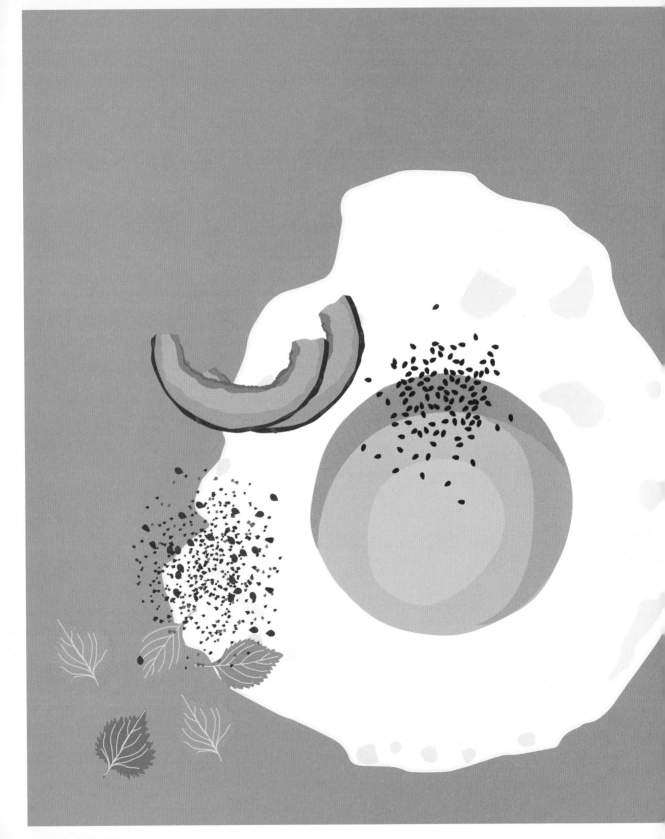

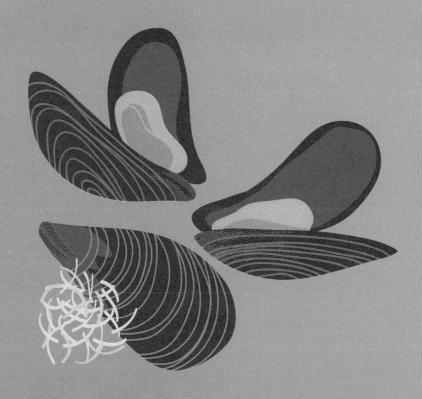

CONTENTS

INTRODUCTION

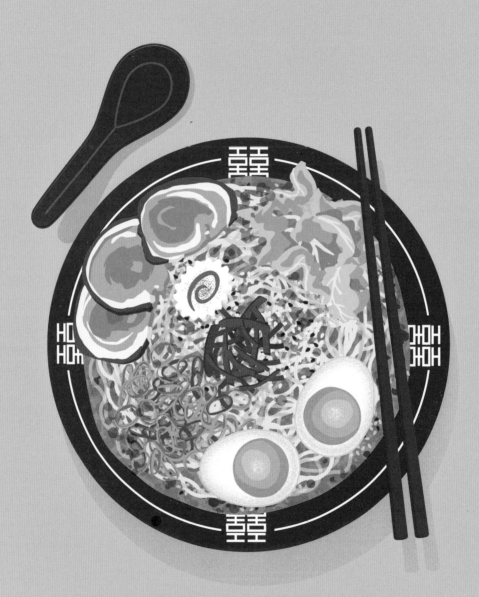

Ramen may have started out as an unassuming and nourishing quick factory worker's meal, but it has evolved. This simple bowl of noodles and broth has been elevated to the status of Japanese cultural icon that now carries a worldwide cult following.

Although history shows that in the 1890s a Chinese-influenced noodle soup (chanpon) made with pork and vegetables was being served in a Nagasaki restaurant, many prefer a different story to the beginning of ramen. The folklore goes something like this: in 1955 on the island of Hokkaido, a factory worker was eating his bowl of miso soup in a Sapporo bar. Still hungry, he asked to have noodles put in his soup, and so miso ramen was born. He started a trend that became a national movement revolving around a few humble ingredients: broth, noodles, meat and vegetables. Soon, other regions and cities picked up the trend, and various styles of ramen developed and evolved according to regional ingredients and palates. The appetite for ramen noodles grew further when in 1958 Mr Momofuku Ando of the Nissin Food Products Company commercialised the production of instant ramen noodles, making them available to everyone. As a result, by the 1970s, the world was eating 'cup noodles' and thinking of them as ramen.

This is a far cry from the elevated status of ramen today where noodle-making techniques are studied, stocks and broths are painstakingly and lovingly conjured and ingredient ideas are pushed beyond simple pork belly or chashu.

Hungry patrons wait in long lines that coil around restaurant buildings, queueing for hours just to get a seat at the bar, where ramen chefs have become ramen masters, possessing the status of rock stars.

The anatomy of a ramen bowl is simple and complex at the same time. It is a matrix of flavours and textures, a crescendo of sensational aromas, wafting together in harmony. At its heart lie the noodles. They may be thin or thick, curly or straight, but they must be firm and springy to the bite and be able to withstand the heat of the broth without becoming soggy. Kansui, known as 'lye water' or 'alkaline water' is made using alkaline salts, and it is this ingredient that gives the noodles their distinctive yellow hue and their texture.

Then there's the broth, with its complex layers of umami flavour. There are four basic styles: shio, which is a salty broth, often made using chicken and fish as a flavour base; tonkotsu, a thick, collagen-rich fatty pork broth, made by boiling pork bones for up to 48 hours; shoyu, which uses soy sauce as its main flavour component and chicken, vegetable and sometimes beef as its stock base; and miso broth, which, as the name suggests, uses copious amounts of miso paste, and often uses a chicken, fish and pork fat base. Within all these broths is the tare, the 'mind' of the soup: a seasoning concoction that delivers the umami layers needed to create an overall balanced taste. The tare may include soy sauce, sake, mirin, salt, garlic, pork fat, dashi and even ground sesame seeds. Each tare is unique to the broth, to the ramen shop and to the region.

The body of the ramen is in the toppings. Classics, such as chashu, *menma*, ajitsuke tamago and nori have stood the test of time, but ramen makers are becoming more adventurous. Now, almost anything goes, allowing you to create your own flavour combinations in every bowl.

So start cooking and be adventurous, experiment with toppings and tares and find your own way through this delicious bowl of comfort food, one slurp at a time.

And in the words of Momofuku Ando:

"Peace will come to the world when people have enough (noodles) to eat."

Peace. Slurp. Ramen.

ESSENTIALS

BEAN SPROUTS
Both mung beans and soya beans are commonly sprouted. Bean sprouts are used in Asian dishes to add a fresh, crisp and crunchy texture.

BLACK MAYU
A burnt garlic and sesame oil. Black mayu creates an added layer of savoury richness when drizzled over ramen dishes.

CHILLI OIL
Chilli-infused oil, or *rayu*, is a condiment commonly used for kicking up the heat and spice levels in Japanese cuisine. Made with toasted sesame oil, corn oil or a blend of oils, this spicy hot oil is a pantry staple. Drizzled across steaming ramen, the oil beads on the broth surface, ensuring that every noodle it touches has a fiery flavour attached.

CORN
Sweetcorn started appearing atop ramen in Hokkaido, Japan's northernmost island, over 20 years ago, where it is farmed along with other staples such as wheat and soybeans. Freshly shucked corn kernels add a sweet and crunchy element to ramen, and can be topped with a knob of butter or a butter bomb.

GARLIC CHIVES
Known as *nira* in Japan, freshly chopped garlic chives make a great addition to ramen adding an herbaceous note, somewhere between garlic and spring onion (scallion). Their blossoms are edible and can also be sprinkled on top of ramen.

GINGER
Fresh ginger adds a punch of heat to warm up any dish and is commonly used in Japanese noodle dishes, soups and marinades.

Beni shoga is julienned ginger that has been pickled in plum vinegar with purple shiso leaves to turn it red. Equally perfect served with a fatty, rich pork ramen or a simple vegetable ramen to cleanse and lift the flavours.

KABOCHA

This Japanese winter squash is also known as Japanese pumpkin. Sweet in flavour, this dense orange-fleshed vegetable can be steamed, grilled or roasted before adding to ramen.

KATSUOBUSHI

Also known as dried bonito flakes, it is an essential ingredient in dashi. Paper-thin shavings of dried smoked bonito, resembling fine wood shavings, deliver a unique yet ubiquitous flavour quintessential to Japanese cooking. Added to soups, stocks and broths or simply used in small amounts as a flavouring garnish, it lends a seriously layered umami rich hit.

KIMCHI

Korean in origin, this spicy dish has crossed many continents and cultures. Made from fermented cabbage, daikon, onion, ginger and lots of chilli powder and garlic, kimchi has a pungent smell and a distinct flavour that is very moreish, and has accrued fans worldwide. Simple to make, add it to your ramen pantry and you won't be disappointed.

MENMA

For many, this Japanese condiment is an acquired taste, yet *menma* is a 'classic' topping in the world of ramen. It is made from lactate fermented bamboo shoots and is available in most Asian supermarkets.

MIRIN

A Japanese sweet rice wine with a delicate subtle flavour, mirin is often used in cooking to marinate meats and fish, masking their strong flavours, and to create shiny glazed sauces, providing an overall balance to many dishes.

MISO

This fermented soya bean paste is commonly made from a combination of soya beans, grains, such as rice or barley, and fermented with *koji*, a yeast used in the making of sake and mirin. There are many varieties of miso paste, all with unique flavours and specific culinary uses. The ingredients used and length of time taken to ferment, determine its final colour and flavour. Two of the most common miso pastes are shiro miso: a young, sweet, white miso paste made from rice, most

often used to marinate vegetables and fish, and for adding to mild-flavoured soups; and aka miso: a reddish-brown miso paste, which is fermented for longer and usually made with barley. It has a rich, salty, intense umami taste and is used for bold-flavoured soups, stews and meats.

MUSHROOMS

Dried or fresh, a wide variety of mushrooms are used to flavour ramen. Dried shiitakes give vegan dashi or soup stock a powerful umami lift, while fresh shiitakes, more delicate in flavour, give a chewy brawny quality to dishes. Enoki, also known as *enokitake* or *enokidake*, are fragile, long, thin white mushrooms. They are used in soups, salads and stir-fries and have a soft, mild flavour. Wood ear, also known as black fungus or cloud ear mushrooms, are available fresh, but are commonly used rehydrated from dried. Subtle in flavour, they have a firm gelatinous texture. King brown mushrooms are part of the oyster mushroom family. Rich in flavour and firm in texture, they are used in sautés and perfect stir-fried and served in ramen.

NOODLES

Ramen noodles are made with wheat flour, water and kansui, an alkaline mineral powder that gives them a yellowish hue and springy bite. Thick or thin, curly or straight, there is a noodle to suit every type of ramen. If you are gluten intolerant, you can substitute rice or kelp noodles.

PONZU

A blend of soy sauce and yuzu juice. Yuzu is a citrus fruit with a mild tang and a lemon—orange flavour. Ponzu is used in marinades, dressings and fish dishes.

RADISH

Daikon is a Japanese white radish with a mild peppery taste. It can be eaten raw, cooked or pickled, and used in salads, soups and to accompany fatty meat dishes, such as pork. Serve pickled alongside a rich pork ramen.

RICE VINEGAR

A mild and mellow vinegar, made from brown or white rice, it is a foundation in Japanese cooking. Use it to make pickles and dressings.

SAKE

A Japanese rice wine and one of the 'holy trinity' of essential ingredients in Japanese cooking, along with soy sauce and mirin. Cooking sake has a lower alcohol content than drinking sake, and is less sweet than mirin. Use in marinades, sauces and tares.

SEAWEEDS

Seaweeds or sea vegetables are rich in vitamins and minerals. They play an ever-present role in Japanese cooking and in the world of ramen. Kombu, also known as kelp or konbu, is deep-green in colour and has a large, wide flat shape. Indispensable in the making of dashi, it can be used in many stocks, stews and condiments, adding a rich umami flavour that delivers a salty seawater essence. Nori, also known as laver, is most commonly used in sushi-making, but has a deserved place in the ramen bowl. Processed into toasted flat sheets, cut into squares and perched inside the bowl, or crumbled and sprinkled on top, it enhances every dish with its mineral-rich flavour. Wakame is soft in texture, mild and almost sweet in flavour and is most commonly used in miso soup. Available dried in long strips, or shredded into small pieces, it easily rehydrates for a quick addition to your ramen of choice.

SESAME SEEDS

Black and white sesame seeds are different varieties from the same plant. Black sesame seeds are unhulled and have a slightly nuttier, more robust taste than white sesame seeds that have been hulled. Both can be toasted to release their aromatic buttery flavour. Used as a garnish for ramen, ground up as tahini for tonkotsu, or in a condiment, such as gomasio, these little seeds are highly versatile.

SHICHIMI TOGARASHI

Also known as nana iro togarashi, this Japanese spice mix has been used for hundreds of years to season soups, noodles and rice dishes. It is a blend of ground dried red chilli, sansho chilli, black and white sesame seeds, orange zest, seaweed and ginger. Sprinkle over your ramen toppings.

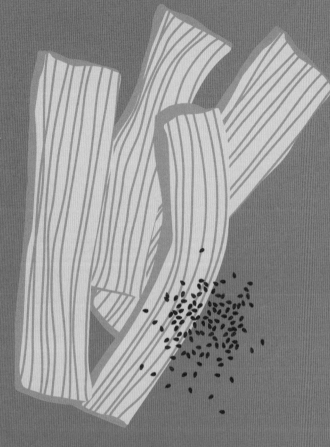

BASICS

MISO BROTH

MAKES ENOUGH FOR 2 BOWLS OF RAMEN

800 ml (27 fl oz) Chicken, Pork and Vegetable stock

1 x quantity Miso Tare

2 teaspoons Rendered Pork Fat (see page 41) or chicken fat

CHICKEN, PORK AND VEGETABLE STOCK

MAKES 2 LITRES (68 FL OZ/8 CUPS)

1 kg (2 lb 3 oz) chicken wings

1 kg (2 lb 3 oz) chicken necks

1 kg (2 lb 3 oz) pork bones, fatty ribs or trotters sawn into quarters by your butcher

2 onions, quartered

1 carrot, quartered

1 leek, quartered

4 dried shiitake mushrooms

6 garlic cloves, smashed

1 teaspoon black peppercorns

30 g (1 oz) ginger, chopped

MISO TARE

100 g (3½ oz/⅓ cup) white miso paste

100 g (3½ oz/⅓ cup) red miso paste

3 garlic cloves, finely grated

2 teaspoons mirin

1 teaspoon toasted sesame oil

pinch of ground white pepper

1 teaspoon tahini (optional)

TO MAKE THE STOCK

Place the chicken wings and necks, and the pork bones, ribs or trotters in a large stockpot. Cover with water and bring to the boil. Blanch for 10 — 15 minutes, then drain, discarding the liquid.

Rinse and scrub the bones of any scum, transfer to a clean stockpot and add the remaining ingredients. Cover with 4.5 litres (4¾ quarts) water, bring to the boil and skim off any impurities that rise to the surface. Reduce the heat, cover and simmer for 2 — 2½ hours until you are left with about 2 litres (68 fl oz/8 cups) liquid.

Strain the stock and discard the solids. Leave to cool before refrigerating. The stock will keep in an airtight container in the fridge for up to 5 days or in the freezer for up to 3 months.

TO MAKE THE TARE

Whisk the ingredients in a small bowl to combine. The tare will keep in an airtight container in the fridge for up to 5 days.

TO MAKE THE BROTH

In a small saucepan, bring the stock to a rapid simmer. Whisk in the miso tare and add the fat.

Serve over ramen noodles with your favourite toppings.

SHOYU BROTH

MAKES ENOUGH FOR 2 BOWLS OF RAMEN

800 ml (27 fl oz), Chicken, Vegetable and Fish stock

1 x quantity Shoyu Tare

1½ tablespoons Rendered Pork Fat (see page 41) or chicken fat

CHICKEN, VEGETABLE AND FISH STOCK

MAKES 2 LITRES (68 FL OZ/8 CUPS)

1 kg (2 lb 3 oz) chicken wings

1 kg (2 lb 3 oz) chicken necks

2 onions, quartered

1 carrot, quartered

1 leek, quartered

4 dried shiitake mushrooms

6 garlic cloves, smashed

1 teaspoon black peppercorns

15 g (½ oz) bonito flakes (katsuobushi)

SHOYU TARE

70 ml (2¼ fl oz) soy sauce

3 teaspoons Dashi Stock (see page 19)

1½ teaspoons sake

1½ teaspoons mirin

1½ teaspoons toasted sesame oil

¼ teaspoon finely grated ginger

⅓ teaspoon finely grated garlic

TO MAKE THE STOCK

Place the chicken wings and necks, vegetables, garlic and peppercorns in a large stockpot and cover with 5 litres (5¼ quarts) water. Bring to the boil and skim off any impurities that rise to the surface. Reduce the heat, cover and simmer for 2 – 2½ hours until you are left with about 2 litres (68 fl oz/8 cups) of stock. Add the bonito flakes, simmer for 5 minutes, then remove from the heat.

Strain the stock and discard the solids.

Leave to cool before refrigerating. The stock will keep in an airtight container in the fridge for up to 5 days or in the freezer for up to 3 months.

TO MAKE THE TARE

Whisk the ingredients in a small bowl to combine. The tare will keep in an airtight container in the fridge for up to 1 week.

TO MAKE THE BROTH

Combine all the ingredients in a saucepan and bring to a simmer, whisking.

Serve over ramen noodles with your favourite toppings.

TONKOTSU BROTH

MAKES ENOUGH FOR 2 BOWLS OF RAMEN

800 ml (27 fl oz) Tonkotsu Stock

1 x quantity Tonkotsu Tare

1½ tablespoons Rendered Pork Fat (see page 41)

TONKOTSU STOCK

MAKES 2 LITRES (68 FL OZ/8 CUPS)

2 kg (4 lb 6 oz) pork thigh bones, sawn into 3 cm (1¼ in) discs by your butcher

2 pig's trotters, sawn in half by your butcher

1 onion, quartered

8 garlic cloves, smashed

TONKOTSU TARE

2 tablespoons Rendered Pork Fat (see page 41)

1½ tablespoons tahini

2 teaspoons soy sauce or chashu cooking liquid (see page 28)

1 teaspoon mirin

1½ teaspoons sea salt

⅛ teaspoon ground white pepper

2 garlic cloves, finely grated

TO MAKE THE STOCK

Place the bones and trotters in a large stockpot and cover with water. Bring to the boil and blanch for 10 — 15 minutes, then drain, discarding the liquid. Rinse and scrub the bones and trotters, removing any brown-coloured bits of blood, as they will discolour the broth.

Return the bones and trotters to a clean stock pot, add 6 litres (6⅓ quarts) water and bring to the boil. Skim off any impurities that rise to the surface, then cover with a lid and boil rapidly for 6 hours, topping up with extra water as needed.

Add the onion and garlic and continue to boil, covered, for a further 2 — 3 hours, topping up with water. Continue to cook until the liquid has reduced to about 2 litres (68 fl oz/8 cups). You should be left with a milky white, collagen-rich thick stock.

Strain the broth and discard the bones and vegetables.

Leave the stock to cool before refrigerating. Store the stock in an airtight container in the fridge for up to 5 days or in the freezer for up to 3 months.

TO MAKE THE TARE

Whisk the ingredients in a small bowl to combine. The tare will keep in an airtight container in the fridge for up to 5 days.

TO MAKE THE BROTH

Combine all the ingredients in a saucepan and bring to a simmer, whisking.

Serve over ramen noodles with your favourite toppings.

SHIO BROTH

MAKES ENOUGH FOR 2 BOWLS OF RAMEN

400 ml (13½ fl oz) Simple Chicken Stock

400 ml (13½ fl oz) Dashi Stock (see page 19)

1 x quantity Shio tare

1½ tablespoons Rendered Pork Fat (see page 41) or chicken fat

SIMPLE CHICKEN STOCK

MAKES 2 LITRES (68 FL OZ/8 CUPS)

1 x 2 kg (4 lb 6 oz) organic whole chicken, rinsed

6 garlic cloves, smashed

½ teaspoon white peppercorns

SHIO TARE

2 tablespoons fine sea salt

1 tablespoon boiling water

2 tablespoons sake

1 tablespoon mirin

2 teaspoons toasted sesame oil

1 teaspoon soy sauce

1 garlic clove, finely grated

TO MAKE THE STOCK

Place the chicken in a large stockpot, cover with 5 litres (5¼ quarts) water and slowly bring to the boil. Skim off any impurities that rise to the surface, then reduce the heat and maintain a slow simmer for about 4 hours, adding the garlic cloves and pepper in the final hour of cooking. You will be left with about 2 litres (68 fl oz/8 cups) stock.

Strain the stock and pick the meat from the bones, reserving it to use in your ramen of choice or in soups or salads.

Leave the stock to cool before refrigerating. It will keep in an airtight container in the fridge for up to 5 days or in the freezer for up to 3 months. If not using rendered pork fat, skim off the fat that solidifies on the surface of the stock and add it to your shio broth.

TO MAKE THE TARE

Place the salt in a bowl, pour over the boiling water and whisk until dissolved.

Add the remaining ingredients and whisk to combine. The tare will keep in an airtight container in the fridge for up to 5 days.

TO MAKE THE BROTH

Combine all the ingredients in a saucepan and bring to a simmer, whisking.

Serve over ramen noodles with your favourite toppings.

VEGAN BROTH

MAKES ENOUGH FOR 2 BOWLS OF RAMEN

800 ml (27 fl oz) Vegan Stock

1 x quantity Vegan Tare

VEGAN STOCK

MAKES 2 LITRES (68 FL OZ/8 CUPS)

1 leek, roughly chopped

2 onions, quartered

2 carrots, roughly chopped

4 spring onions (scallions)

3 teaspoon peanut oil

6 dried shiitake mushrooms

6 garlic cloves, smashed

20 g (¾ oz) ginger, chopped

½ teaspoon white peppercorns

15 g (½ oz) kombu

VEGAN TARE

100 g (3½ oz/⅓ cup) red miso paste

2 tablespoons tahini

1 tablespoon soy sauce

1 tablespoon mirin

1 tablespoon sake

1 tablespoon ponzu

2 teaspoons toasted sesame oil

1 garlic clove, finely grated

½ teaspoon finely grated ginger

TO MAKE THE STOCK

Rinse the leek to remove any grit. Transfer to a bowl along with the onion, carrot, spring onions and oil. Toss well to combine. Place in a large saucepan over medium — high heat and slightly char the vegetables to deepen their flavour. Add the mushrooms, garlic, ginger and peppercorns. Cover with 4 litres (4¼ quarts) water and bring to the boil. Reduce to a rapid simmer and cook for 1 — 1½ hours until reduced to about 2 litres (68 fl oz/8 cups) of stock. Add the kombu, simmer for 5 minutes, then remove from the heat and leave to infuse in the stock for 15 — 20 minutes.

Strain the stock, reserving the mushrooms to make Pickled Shiitake Mushrooms (see page 37) and the kombu to make Tsukudani (see page 38), if you like. Discard the remaining solids.

Leave to cool before refrigerating. The stock will keep in an airtight container in the fridge for up to 5 days or in the freezer for up to 3 months.

TO MAKE THE TARE

Whisk the ingredients in a small bowl to combine. The tare will keep in an airtight container in the fridge for up to 5 days.

TO MAKE THE BROTH

Combine the ingredients in a small saucepan and bring to a simmer.

Serve over ramen, rice or kelp noodles with your favourite toppings.

DASHI STOCK

MAKES 1 LITRE (34 FL OZ/4 CUPS)

15 g (½ oz) kombu

15 g (½ oz) bonito flakes (*katsuobushi*)

Place the kombu in a large bowl, cover with 1 litre (34 fl oz/ 4 cups) water and set aside in the fridge for 2 — 3 hours or overnight.

Transfer the liquid to a saucepan over low heat and gently heat to 80°C (175°F) — this should take at least 20 minutes. Simmer at this temperature for 5 minutes, then add the bonito flakes and steep for 5 minutes, keeping the temperature at 80°C. Remove from the heat, strain the liquid and discard the solids.

Leave the stock to cool before refrigerating. It will keep in an airtight container in the fridge for up to 5 days.

VEGAN DASHI STOCK

MAKES 1 LITRE (34 FL OZ/4 CUPS)

15 g (½ oz) kombu *sea weed*

5 — 6 dried shiitake mushrooms

Place the kombu and mushrooms in a large bowl, cover with 1 litre (34 fl oz/4 cups) water and set aside in the fridge for 2 — 3 hours or overnight.

Transfer the liquid to a saucepan over low heat and gently heat to 80°C (175°F) — this should take at least 20 minutes. Simmer at this temperature for 5 minutes, then steep for 5 minutes, keeping the temperature at 80°C. Remove from the heat and strain the liquid. Keep the kombu for making Tsukudani (see page 38), if desired and reserve the shiitakes for your ramen or for pickling (see page 37).

Leave the stock to cool before refrigerating. It will keep in an airtight container in the fridge for up to 5 days.

RAMEN NOODLES

MAKES 6 X 120 G (4½ OZ) PORTIONS

1 teaspoon kansui (sodium carbonate powder) (see note)

1 teaspoon fine sea salt

500 g (1 lb 2 oz) 00 flour, plus extra for dusting

Dissolve the kansui and salt in 220 ml (7½ fl oz) water at room temperature.

Place the flour in an electric mixer with a dough hook attachment and mix on low speed while slowly adding the water solution. Mix for 9 — 10 minutes, increasing the speed slightly towards the end, until you have a very crumbly, pebble-like dough. Transfer to a kitchen bench lightly dusted with flour and knead for 2 — 3 minutes. Bring the dough together and shape into a flat disc. Cover with plastic wrap and set aside in the fridge for 30 — 40 minutes to soften.

Lightly dust the kitchen bench with flour. Cut the dough into six even-sized pieces. Working with one piece of dough at a time, and keeping the rest covered, roll the dough through a pasta machine on its widest setting. Fold the dough on top of itself so that it's a double layer and pass through the rollers again. Reduce the width of the rollers to their next setting and roll the dough through. Fold the dough onto itself again and pass through the machine a second time. Repeat this process again on the third widest setting, then continue to pass through the machine reducing the width settings, but without folding the dough onto itself. For thin noodles, roll out the dough until it is 1.5 mm (1⁄16 in) thick, then cut into noodles with the capellini attachment. For thicker noodles, roll out the dough until it is 2 mm (1⁄8 in) thick and cut into noodles with the spaghetti attachment.

Cook the noodles in a large saucepan of boiling salted water for 45 — 55 seconds. Drain well, shaking off the excess water, then transfer to serving bowls. Top with your broth and toppings of choice, and slurp away!

The noodles should be eaten the same day they are made.

NOTE

Kansui is an alkaline powder that gives the noodles their light yellowish colour and chewy texture. It can be found in Asian supermarkets.

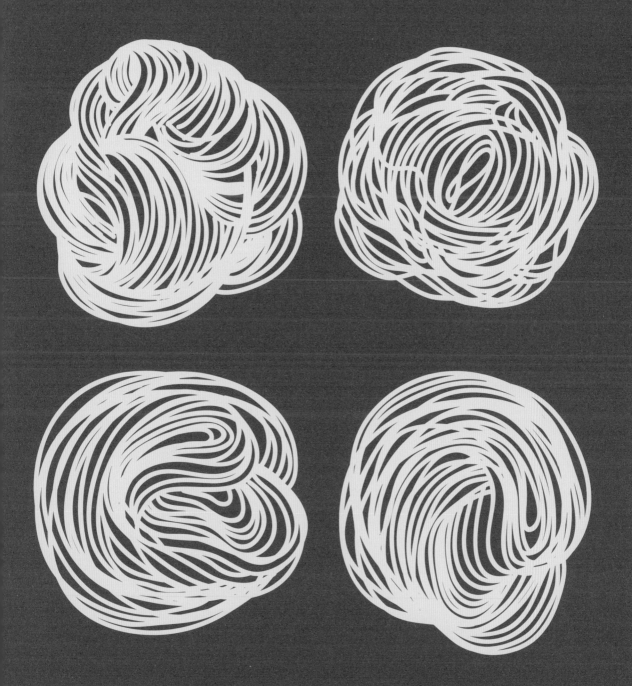

LAKSA PASTE

MAKES ABOUT 375 G (13 OZ/1½ CUPS)

1 teaspoon shrimp paste

1 teaspoon dried shrimp

2 tablespoons peanut oil

20 g (¾ oz) candle nuts or macadamia nuts

150 g (5½ oz) Asian shallots, chopped

3 bird's eye chillies, chopped, seeds removed if desired

3 long red chillies, chopped

4 garlic cloves, peeled

6 coriander (cilantro) sprigs with roots attached, roots well-washed, leaves reserved for garnish

1 lemongrass stalk, white part only, chopped

zest of 1 lime

3 teaspoons freshly grated galangal or ginger

3 teaspoons freshly grated turmeric

1 teaspoon ground coriander

peanut oil

Preheat the oven to 200°C (400°F).

Wrap the shrimp paste and dried shrimp in foil and roast in the oven for 2 — 3 minutes. Allow to cool slightly then unwrap and transfer to a food processor along with the remaining paste ingredients except the peanut oil. Blitz to a fine paste, loosening with a little peanut oil if necessary. Transfer to a large enough jar and cover the paste with oil.

Laksa paste will keep in an airtight container in the fridge for up to 2 weeks.

THAI GREEN CURRY PASTE

MAKES ABOUT 250 G (9 OZ/1 CUP)

1 teaspoon coriander seeds

1 teaspoon cumin seeds

1 teaspoon shrimp paste

½ teaspoon white peppercorns

8 large green chillies, chopped

10 small green chillies, chopped

2 Asian shallots, chopped

3 garlic cloves, chopped

3 teaspoons freshly grated galangal
or ginger

1 teaspoon freshly grated turmeric

1 lemongrass stalk, white part only,
chopped

zest and juice of 1 kaffir lime

2 kaffir lime leaves, shredded

4 coriander (cilantro) roots, cleaned
and chopped

1 teaspoon salt

peanut oil

Preheat the oven to 200°C (400°F).

Heat a small frying pan over medium heat and toast the coriander
and cumin seeds until fragrant. Remove from the heat and grind in
a mortar and pestle.

Wrap the shrimp paste in foil and roast for 2 — 3 minutes. Set
aside to cool a little, then transfer to a food processor along with
the ground coriander and cumin seeds and remaining curry paste
ingredients except the peanut oil. Blend to a paste, loosening with
a little peanut oil if necessary, then transfer to a large enough jar
and cover the paste with oil.

Thai green curry paste will keep in an airtight container in the
fridge for up to 1 week.

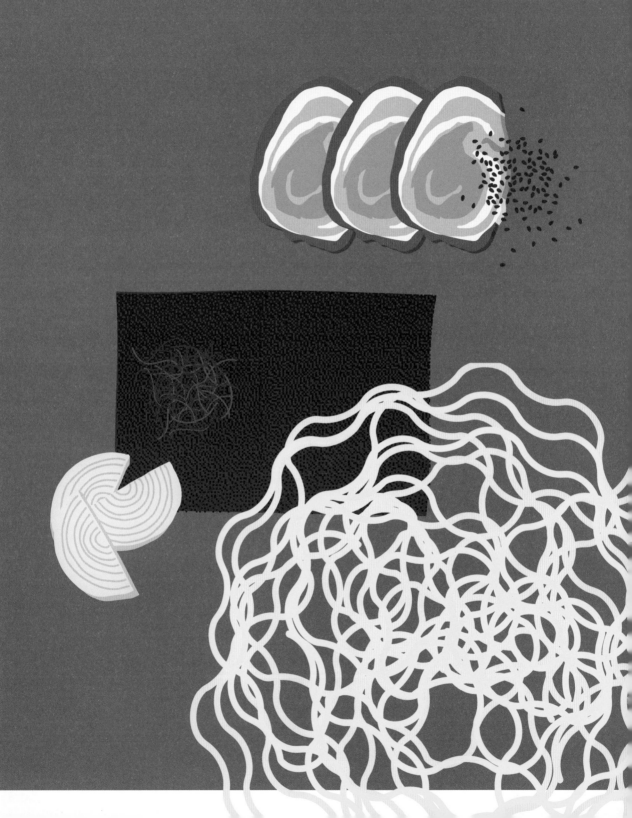

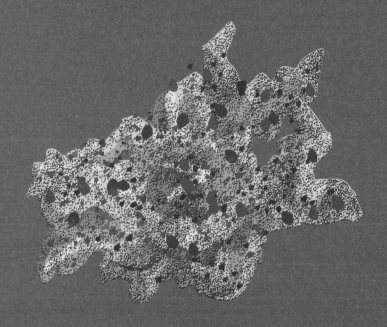

TOPPINGS
AND EXTRAS

AJITSUKE TAMAGO

SEASONED EGGS

MAKES 4 PORTIONS

4 eggs

125 ml (4 fl oz/½ cup) soy sauce

60 ml (2 fl oz/¼ cup) mirin

60 ml (2 fl oz/¼ cup) sake

3 teaspoons caster (superfine) sugar

1 garlic clove, smashed

Place the eggs in a saucepan of boiling water and boil for 6 minutes. Drain and plunge into an ice bath.

Meanwhile, combine the remaining ingredients in a saucepan over medium heat and simmer for 1 — 2 minutes until the sugar dissolves. Remove from the heat, transfer to a heatproof bowl and set aside to cool completely.

Peel the eggs and place them in the cooled soy sauce liquid. Refrigerate for 4 — 5 hours and up to 12 hours. The longer you leave the eggs, the stronger the flavour will be.

Cut the eggs in half, and serve them on your ramen of choice. You can either discard the liquid or use it to season your ramen.

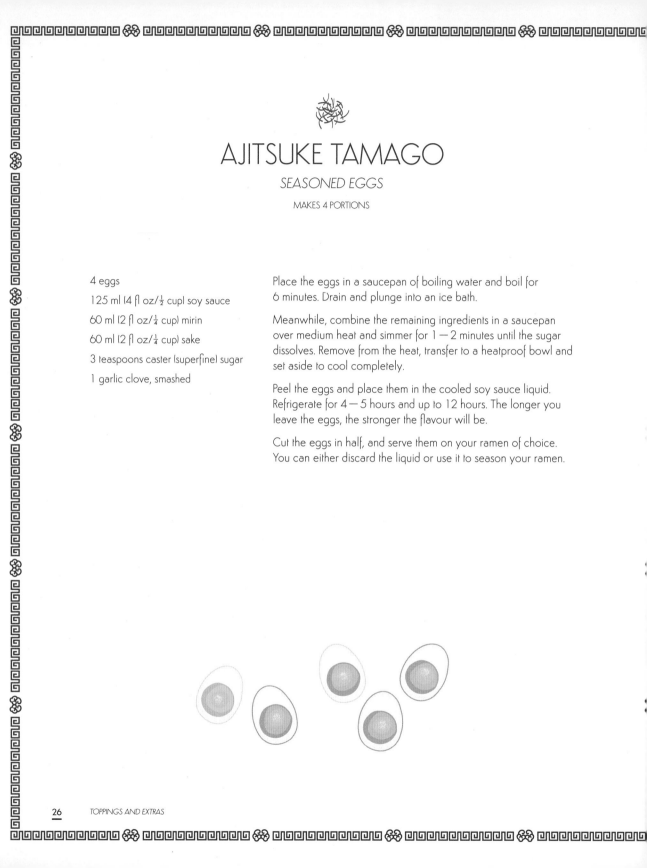

ONSEN TAMAGO

HOT SPRINGS EGGS

MAKES 4 PORTIONS

4 eggs, at room temperature

2 tablespoons mirin

1 teaspoon caster (superfine) sugar

125 ml (4 fl oz/½ cup) light soy sauce

250 ml (8½ fl oz/1 cup) cold Dashi Stock (see page 19)

1 spring onion (scallion), thinly sliced

Using a digital thermometer to assist you, heat a large saucepan of water to exactly 75°C (165°F). Place the eggs in the pan and cook at this temperature for 13 minutes. Transfer to an ice bath to stop the cooking process.

Meanwhile, combine the mirin, sugar and soy sauce in a saucepan over medium heat and simmer for 1 — 2 minutes until the sugar dissolves.

Pour the mirin mixture into the dashi stock and stir to combine. Divide the liquid among four small bowls, add a peeled egg and garnish with a little spring onion. Serve alongside your ramen of choice.

CHASHU PORK

MAKES 8 PORTIONS

1 kg (2 lb 3 oz) boneless pork belly, skin on

250 ml (8½ fl oz/1 cup) sake

250 ml (8½ fl oz/1 cup) mirin

125 ml (4 fl oz/½ cup) soy sauce

125 ml (4 fl oz/½ cup) caster (superfine) sugar

4 spring onions (scallions), quartered

2 Asian shallots, halved

6 garlic cloves, smashed

20 g (¾ oz) ginger, sliced

Preheat the oven to 135°C (275°F).

Roll up the pork belly with the skin on the outside and tie with kitchen string at 2 cm (¾ in) intervals along the pork.

Place the remaining ingredients and 500 ml (17 fl oz/2 cups) water in a Dutch oven and bring to the boil. Remove from the heat and add the pork. Cover and transfer to the oven for 4 — 5 hours, turning the pork occasionally, until completely cooked through and tender.

Cool the pork and the liquid to room temperature, then cover, and transfer the lot to the fridge and leave to rest overnight to achieve maximum flavour.

Remove the pork from the liquid and thinly slice. Serve the chashu on your ramen of choice.

The liquid can be used as the Ajitsuke Tamago marinade (see page 26) or as a tare seasoning for your ramen.

The sliced chashu and liquid will keep in airtight containers in the fridge for 5 — 6 days.

SHREDDED PORK SHOULDER

MAKES 8 PORTIONS

1.5 kg (3 lb 5 oz) pork shoulder, bone in, skin removed

500 ml (17 fl oz/2 cups) chicken stock

250 ml (8½ fl oz/1 cup) soy sauce

2 tablespoons toasted sesame oil

4 garlic cloves, crushed

20 g (¾ oz) ginger, sliced

DRY RUB

2 teaspoons sea salt

2 teaspoons cracked black pepper

2 teaspoons brown sugar

2½ teaspoons Japanese chilli seasoning (shichimi togarashi)

Combine the dry rub ingredients in a bowl and massage over the pork shoulder.

Transfer the pork to a slow cooker and add the remaining ingredients. Cover, and cook on low for about 8 hours, until the pork comes away easily from the bone when tested with a fork. Remove the meat from the slow cooker and shred with two forks.

Serve the pork on your ramen of choice and use the braising liquid as a spicy tare.

The shredded pork and braising liquid will keep in airtight containers in the fridge for 5—6 days or in the freezer for up to 3 months.

You can also remove the fat that solidifies on top of the braising liquid to use in your ramen for that extra fat flavour bomb.

KAKUNI

BRAISED PORK BELLY

MAKES 4 PORTIONS

1 kg (2 lb 3 oz) pork belly, cut into 5 cm (2 in) cubes

30 g (1 oz) ginger, sliced

½ onion, quartered

2 spring onions (scallions), quartered

½ teaspoon sea salt

BRAISING LIQUID

500 ml (17 fl oz/2 cups) Dashi Stock (see page 19)

125 ml (4 fl oz/½ cup) sake

80 ml (2½ fl oz/⅓ cup) soy sauce

60 ml (2 fl oz/¼ cup) mirin

15 g (½ oz) ginger, sliced

2 tablespoons brown sugar

Sear the pork belly cubes in a large frying pan over medium—high heat until golden brown on all sides.

Transfer to a saucepan and add the ginger, onion, spring onion, salt and 2 litres (68 fl oz/8 cups) water and bring to the boil. Reduce to a simmer and cook for 2½—3 hours until the pork is cooked through and tender. Remove the pork from the pan and discard the cooking liquid.

Place all the braising ingredients in a clean saucepan over medium—low heat and add the pork. Simmer for 50—60 minutes until meltingly tender. There should be about 250 ml (8½ fl oz/1 cup) liquid remaining. Remove the pork from the liquid and serve on your ramen of choice.

The remaining braising liquid can be used as a tare to flavour your ramen broth, if you like.

The pork will keep in an airtight container in the fridge for 5—6 days.

VEGETABLE GYOZA

MAKES 25

2 teaspoons toasted sesame oil

peanut oil

100 g (3½ oz) mixed mushrooms, such as shiitake, wood ear and king brown, finely chopped

100 g (3½ oz) cabbage, finely shredded

100 g (3½ oz) firm tofu, crumbled

2 spring onions (scallions), thinly sliced

1 bird's eye chilli, seeds removed and thinly sliced

1 tablespoon finely grated ginger

2 garlic cloves, finely grated

¼ teaspoon ground white pepper

½ teaspoon sea salt

2 teaspoons soy sauce

2 teaspoons sake

1 teaspoon toasted sesame oil

1 egg white

25 gyoza wrappers

Heat the sesame oil and 1 teaspoon peanut oil in a wok over medium heat.

Add the mushrooms and cabbage and sauté for 1 — 2 minutes. Transfer to a heatproof bowl and set aside to cool. Add the remaining ingredients except the wrappers and mix to combine.

Place a scant tablespoon of filling onto a gyoza wrapper and lightly brush half the edges with water. Fold over and crimp, making 4 — 5 pleats to seal. Repeat with the remaining filling and wrappers.

Place 2 tablespoons of peanut oil in a frying pan over medium — high heat. Working in batches, add the gyoza, frying on one side for 2 — 3 minutes, until the bottoms turn golden brown. Add 3 tablespoons water to the pan, cover immediately and steam for about 3 minutes or until the water has evaporated. Repeat with the remaining gyoza, adding more peanut oil as necessary.

Serve hot, either in your ramen of choice or alongside.

Any remaining uncooked gyoza will keep in an airtight container, layered between baking paper, in the freezer for up to 3 months.

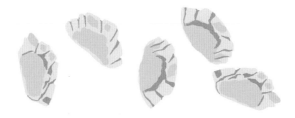

SEAFOOD GYOZA

MAKES 25

Ravioli ?

300 g (10½ oz) raw prawn (shrimp) meat, roughly chopped

20 g (¾ oz) garlic chives, roughly chopped

1 tablespoon sake

1 tablespoon soy sauce

1 teaspoon toasted sesame oil

1½ tablespoons grated ginger

2 garlic cloves, grated

⅓ teaspoon sea salt

pinch of ground white pepper

1 egg white

25 gyoza wrappers

peanut oil, for frying

Place all the ingredients except the gyoza wrappers and peanut oil in a food processor and pulse until combined.

Place a scant tablespoon of filling onto a gyoza wrapper and lightly brush half the edges with water. Fold over and crimp, making 4 — 5 pleats to seal. Repeat with the remaining filling and wrappers.

Place 2 tablespoons of peanut oil in a frying pan over medium — high heat. Working in batches, add the gyoza, frying on one side for 2 — 3 minutes, until the bottoms turn golden brown. Add 3 tablespoons water to the pan, cover immediately and steam for about 3 minutes or until the water has evaporated. Repeat with the remaining gyoza, adding more peanut oil as necessary.

Serve hot, either in your ramen of choice or alongside.

Any remaining uncooked gyoza will keep in an airtight container, layered between baking paper, in the freezer for up to 3 months.

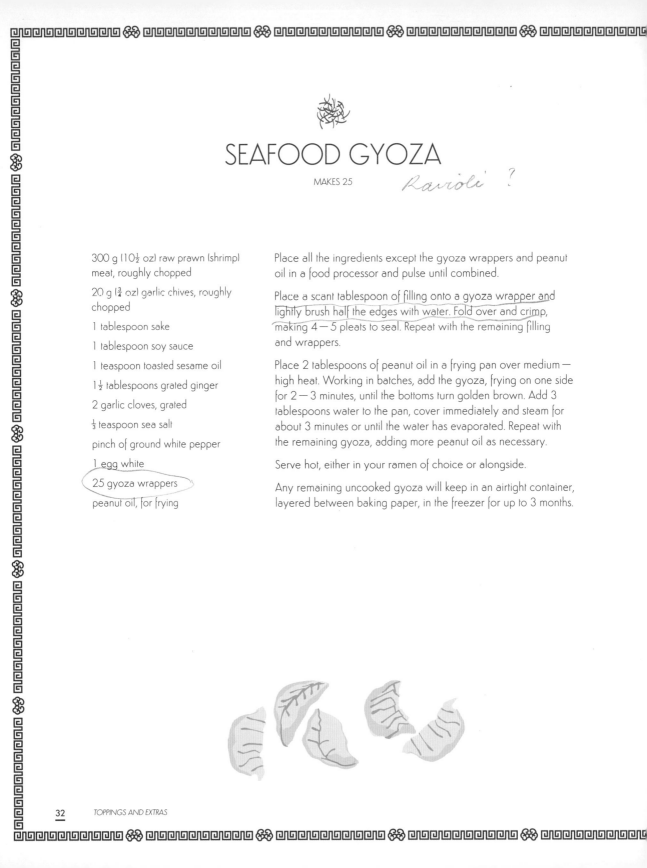

PORK GYOZA

MAKES 25

200 g (7 oz) minced (ground) pork

100 g (3½ oz) cabbage, finely shredded

2 spring onions (scallions), thinly sliced

1½ tablespoons finely grated ginger

2 garlic cloves, finely grated

½ teaspoon cracked black pepper

½ teaspoon sea salt

1 teaspoon toasted sesame oil

1 egg white

25 gyoza wrappers

peanut oil, for frying

Place all the ingredients except the gyoza wrappers and peanut oil in a bowl and mix to combine.

Place a scant tablespoon of filling onto a gyoza wrapper and lightly brush half the edges with water. Fold over and crimp, making 4 — 5 pleats to seal. Repeat with the remaining filling and wrappers.

Place 2 tablespoons of peanut oil in a frying pan over medium — high heat. Working in batches, add the gyoza, frying on one side for 2 — 3 minutes, until the bottoms turn golden brown. Add 3 tablespoons water to the pan, cover immediately and steam for about 3 minutes or until the water has evaporated. Repeat with the remaining gyoza, adding more peanut oil as necessary.

Serve hot, either in your ramen of choice or alongside.

Any remaining uncooked gyoza will keep in an airtight container, layered between baking paper, in the freezer for up to 3 months.

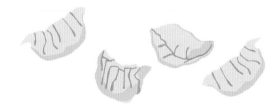

NARUTOMAKI

FISHCAKES

MAKES 16 X 1 CM (½ IN) SLICES

250 g (9 oz) skinless white fish fillet, pin-boned and roughly chopped

1 teaspoon fine sea salt

1 teaspoon caster (superfine) sugar

1 teaspoon mirin

1 egg white

pinch of ground white pepper

3 — 4 drops red food colouring

Place the fish in a bowl of cold water, soak for 3 — 4 minutes, then rinse and drain well, squeezing out any excess water.

Transfer to a food processor along with the salt, sugar, mirin, egg white and pepper, and process to a fine paste.

Cover a bamboo sushi mat with plastic wrap. Using a spatula, spread out three-quarters of the fish mixture on top of the plastic wrap to form an 18 cm x 12 cm (7 in x 4¾ in) rectangle. Mix the food colouring into the remaining fish mixture and spread this on top.

Carefully roll the sushi mat away from you to form the narutomaki into a log shape. Tightly twist the ends of the plastic wrap to encase the mixture.

Bring a large saucepan of water to the boil and place a bamboo steamer over the top. Place the narutomaki in the steamer and steam for about 20 minutes, until cooked through.

Leave to cool to room temperature, before slicing into 1 cm (½ in) pieces and adding to your ramen of choice.

Narutomaki will keep in an airtight container in the fridge for up to 5 days or in the freezer for up to 3 months.

KIMCHI

MAKES 1 LITRE (34 FL OZ/4 CUPS)

1 kg (2 lb 3 oz) wombok (Chinese cabbage), sliced into 4 cm (1½ in) strips

80 g (2¾ oz) sea salt

1.5 litres (51 fl oz/6 cups) filtered water

5 garlic cloves, finely grated

30 g (1 oz) ginger, finely grated

200 g (7 oz) daikon, julienned

4 spring onions (scallions), thinly sliced

1 tablespoon dried shrimp (see note)

3 tablespoons Korean chilli powder (gochugaru)

2 tablespoons soy sauce

2 tablespoons fish sauce

Place the cabbage in a large glass bowl and sprinkle over the salt. Using your hands, rub the salt into the cabbage. Cover with the filtered water and leave to macerate for 2 — 3 hours. Drain and rinse the cabbage, and squeeze out any remaining water.

Place the cabbage back in the glass bowl and mix in the garlic, ginger, daikon, spring onion and dried shrimp.

In a small bowl, mix together the chilli powder, soy sauce and fish sauce, then pour over the cabbage mixture and thoroughly combine (use gloves if mixing by hand). Taste, and add more chilli, if desired.

Tightly pack the kimchi into a 1 litre (34 fl oz/4 cup) sterilised jar — the mixture should be completely submerged in the liquid. Add water if necessary, then seal and leave at room temperature, out of direct sunlight, to ferment for 1 — 5 days. The longer you leave the kimchi, the stronger the flavour will be. Transfer to the fridge where it will keep for 4 — 5 months.

Serve the kimchi either in your ramen of choice or alongside.

NOTE

To make vegan kimchi, omit the dried shrimp and fish sauce and replace with 2 tablespoons dulse flakes or one finely ground nori sheet.

GARLIC CHIPS

MAKES ABOUT 50 G (1¾ OZ/½ CUP) GARLIC CHIPS AND ABOUT 140 ML (4½ FL OZ) GARLIC OIL

1 head of garlic (about 50 g/1¾ oz), peeled

170 ml (5½ fl oz/⅔ cup) peanut oil

2 teaspoons toasted sesame oil

Thinly slice the garlic cloves lengthwise, evenly and uniformly, so they are all the same thickness — this will ensure even cooking.

Heat the oils and garlic in a frying pan over low heat and slowly fry the garlic for 6—7 minutes until golden and crisp. Remove from the oil and drain on paper towels, reserving the oil.

The garlic chips will keep in an airtight container for 1—2 days, but they are best used the same day.

The garlic oil will keep in a sealed jar in the fridge for about 2 months.

WAKAME GOMASIO

MAKES ABOUT 180 G (6½ OZ/1½ CUPS)

155 g (5½ oz/1 cup) sesame seeds

1 piece (6—7 g/¼ oz) dried wakame

2 tablespoons sea salt flakes

Preheat the oven to 160°C (320°F).

Toast the sesame seeds in a heavy-based frying pan over very low heat for 5—6 minutes until they take on a deep golden brown colour and a buttery aroma. Remove from the pan and set aside to cool completely.

Place the wakame on a baking tray and toast in the oven for 9—10 minutes. Set aside to cool completely.

Transfer the sesame seeds, wakame and the salt to a food processor and pulse for about 30 seconds, until the ingredients are quite finely ground but still with a few whole seeds.

Sprinkle wakame gomasio over your favourite ramen toppings or blend into your broth of choice.

Store in a sealed jar in the pantry for up to 3 weeks.

FURIKAKE

MAKES ABOUT 80 G (2¾ OZ)

40 g (1½ oz/¼ cup) sesame seeds

2 tablespoons black sesame seeds

3 nori sheets

4 g (¼ oz/¼ cup) bonito flakes (*katsuobushi*)

2 teaspoons sea salt flakes

1 teaspoon caster (superfine) sugar (optional)

Toast the sesame seeds in a heavy-based frying pan over very low heat for 5 — 6 minutes until they take on a deep golden brown colour and a buttery aroma. Remove from the pan and set aside to cool completely.

Transfer all the ingredients to a food processor and pulse to blend.

Sprinkle furikake over rice or your ramen of choice.

Store in a sealed jar in the pantry for 1 — 2 months.

PICKLED SHIITAKE MUSHROOMS

MAKES ABOUT 230 G (8 OZ)

125 ml (4 fl oz/½ cup) soy sauce or tamari

125 ml (4 fl oz/½ cup) rice wine vinegar

55 g (2 oz/¼ cup) caster (superfine) sugar

3 thin slices ginger, peeled

1 small red chilli, sliced in half

230 g (8 oz) rehydrated shiitake mushrooms

Place the soy sauce, rice wine vinegar, 125 ml (4 fl oz/½ cup) water, sugar, ginger and chilli in a small saucepan over low — medium heat and whisk until the sugar dissolves.

Place the mushrooms in a heatproof bowl and pour the pickling liquid over the top. Set aside to cool then refrigerate.

The mushrooms will be ready to use in about 3 hours, and will keep in an airtight container in the fridge for 1 week.

Serve alongside pork dishes, ramen and cold noodle salads.

JAPANESE QUICK PICKLES

MAKES ABOUT 680 ML (23 FL OZ)

175 g (6 oz/1½ cups) finely sliced radishes

1 umeboshi plum

1 small red chilli, halved

½ garlic clove, sliced (optional)

250 ml (8½ fl oz/1 cup) rice wine vinegar

2 tablespoons caster (superfine) sugar

2 teaspoons fine sea salt

5 black peppercorns

Place the radish, plum, chilli and garlic, if using, in a heatproof bowl.

Heat the rice wine vinegar, 250 ml (8½ fl oz/1 cup) water, sugar, salt and peppercorns in a saucepan over medium heat. Stir to dissolve the sugar and salt and bring to the boil. Pour over the sliced vegetables and leave to cool.

Serve alongside pork dishes, ramen and cold noodle salads.

The pickles will keep in an airtight container in the fridge for up to 1 week.

Try pickling other vegetables too, such as cucumber, cabbage or daikon, or a combination.

TSUKUDANI

SWEET BRAISED KOMBU

sea weed MAKES ABOUT 45 G (1½ OZ)

2 large pieces kombu (about 6.5 cm x 17.5 cm/2½ in x 7 in each) julienned (or use rehydrated kombu from Dashi Stock; see page 19)

2 tablespoons soy sauce

3 teaspoons rice wine vinegar

1 tablespoon mirin

1½ tablespoons caster (superfine) sugar

250 ml (8½ fl oz/1 cup) Dashi Stock (see page 19)

1 teaspoon toasted sesame seeds

Place the kombu in a saucepan and add the soy sauce, rice wine vinegar, mirin, sugar and dashi. Bring to the boil, then reduce to a simmer and cook for 25 — 35 minutes, until the mixture reduces to a thick sticky glaze, just coating the kombu.

Sprinkle in the sesame seeds and stir through.

Serve alongside rice, ramen or pork dishes.

It will keep in a sealed jar in the fridge for up to 1 week.

MISO BUTTER BOMB

MAKES ABOUT 390 G (14 OZ)

250 g (9 oz) butter, softened

135 g (5 oz) white miso paste

2 garlic cloves, finely grated

1 teaspoon ponzu

Place all the ingredients in a food processor and blitz to combine.

Chill in the fridge, then roll into small balls (bombs) to add to your ramen. It can also be rolled into a log shape and encased in baking paper or plastic wrap, and kept in the freezer for up to 3 months. Slice off portions as required and melt over corn in ramen or vegetables and fish.

SEAWEED BUTTER BOMB

MAKES ABOUT 280 G (10 OZ)

2 nori sheets, crumbled

250 g (9 oz) butter, softened or Rendered Pork Fat (see page 41)

1 teaspoon lemon zest

2 garlic cloves, finely grated

1 teaspoon toasted sesame seeds

½ teaspoon Japanese chilli seasoning (*shichimi togarashi*) (see note)

¼ teaspoon toasted sesame oil

¼ teaspoon soy sauce

Transfer the nori sheets to a food processor and pulse until finely chopped. Add the remaining ingredients and blitz to combine.

Chill in the fridge, then roll into small balls (bombs) to add to your ramen. It can also be rolled into a log shape and encased in baking paper or plastic wrap, and kept in the freezer for up to 3 months. Slice off portions as required and melt over corn in ramen or vegetables and fish.

NOTE
Shichimi togarashi can be purchased from most Asian supermarkets.

UMAMI MUSHROOM POWDER

MAKES 85 G (3 OZ/⅔ CUP)

20 g (¾ oz) dried shiitake mushrooms

40 g (1½ oz/⅓ cup) sea salt flakes

1 tablespoon Korean chilli powder (gochugaru)

½ teaspoon black peppercorns

Place all the ingredients in a spice grinder and pulverise to a powder.

Sprinkle over ramen, eggs, veggies ... Everything, for a spiced umami hit.

Store in a glass jar in the pantry for up to 6 months.

BLACK MAYU

BLACK GARLIC OIL

MAKES ABOUT 160 ML (5½ FL OZ)

80 ml (2½ fl oz/⅓ cup) peanut oil

1 head of garlic, peeled and chopped

80 ml (2½ fl oz/⅓ cup) toasted sesame oil

1 tablespoon toasted black sesame seeds

pinch of salt

Heat the peanut oil and garlic in a frying pan over medium heat. Cook slowly until the garlic starts to brown. Reduce the heat to low and continue cooking for 7 — 8 minutes, until the garlic blackens. Remove from the heat, add the sesame oil and process in a blender with the sesame seeds and salt until smooth. Allow to cool before straining through a fine sieve into a jar.

Drizzle over your ramen of choice.

The mayu will keep in an airtight container in the fridge for 1½ — 2 months.

RENDERED PORK FAT

MAKES ABOUT 260 G (9 OZ/11/4 CUPS)

500 g (1 lb 2 oz) organic pork fat,
cut into 3 cm (1¼ in) cubes

Place the fat and 125 ml (4 fl oz/½ cup) water in a heavy-based saucepan and cook over low heat for 4 – 5 hours. Occasionally stir the fat and ensure that the heat is gentle enough to melt the fat instead of charring and burning it. During this time the water will evaporate and the fat will very slowly render into liquid, leaving behind small, golden brown chunks of fat. Drain the liquid through a fine-meshed sieve into a sterilised jar and discard the solids. The liquid will be a light yellowish colour but will change to pure white when solidified. Alternatively, cook the fat in a slow cooker, covered, on low for 7 – 8 hours.

Store in an airtight container in the fridge for up to 3 months or in the freezer for up to 6 months.

Use in ramen broths and tares, and to fry with.

MISO RAMEN

BUTTERED CORN, BACON AND
AJITSUKE TAMAGO MISO RAMEN

SERVES 2

4 slices smoked bacon

2 portions thick Ramen Noodles (see page 20), cooked al dente and drained

800 ml (27 fl oz) Miso Broth (see page 14), simmering

2 Ajitsuke Tamago (see page 26), halved

10 slices fermented bamboo shoots (menma)

100 g (3½ oz) fresh corn kernels, blanched

2 Miso Butter Bombs (see page 39) *NO*

2 spring onions (scallions), finely sliced

2 teaspoons toasted black sesame seeds *No*

Put the bacon in a cold cast-iron frying pan and place over medium — high heat (this renders the bacon evenly). Fry for about 8 minutes until well cooked and crisp, then chop into bite-sized pieces.

To assemble the ramen, quickly and evenly divide the warm drained noodles between two bowls and pour over the hot miso broth. Add the bacon, ajitsuke tamago, bamboo shoots and corn. Dot the corn with a miso butter bomb and garnish with spring onion and sesame seeds. Drizzle some of the bacon fat from the pan over the ramen for extra flavour and serve straight away.

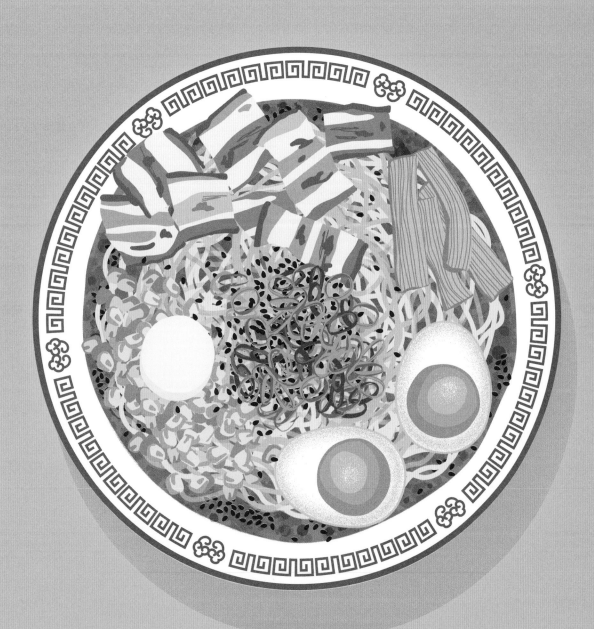

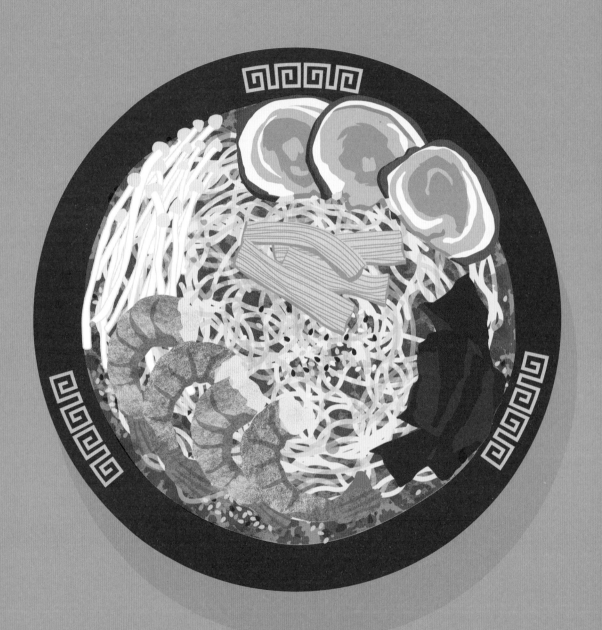

SPICY PRAWN, CHASHU PORK AND ENOKI MUSHROOM MISO RAMEN

SERVES 2

8 raw prawns (shrimp), shelled with tails left intact, deveined

1 tablespoon peanut oil

6 slices Chashu Pork (see page 28)

800 ml (27 fl oz) Miso Broth (see page 14), simmering

2 portions thick Ramen Noodles (see page 20), cooked al dente and drained

30 g (1 oz) enoki mushrooms

10 slices fermented bamboo shoots (*menma*)

2 teaspoons toasted sesame seeds

3 teaspoons shio kombu (see note)

PRAWN SAUCE

2 teaspoons finely grated ginger

1 garlic clove, finely grated

1 spring onion (scallion), finely sliced

1 — 2 tablespoons spicy chilli bean paste (*la doubanjiang*), to taste (see note)

2 teaspoons rice wine vinegar

1 teaspoon toasted sesame oil

To make the prawn sauce, combine the ingredients in a bowl and mix well. Add the prawns and toss well to coat.

Heat the oil in a frying pan over medium heat, add the prawns and fry for 2 — 3 minutes until just cooked. Remove from the heat and keep warm.

Place the chashu slices into the simmering broth to gently warm, or warm through in the chashu braising liquid.

To assemble the ramen, quickly and evenly divide the warm drained noodles between two bowls and pour over the hot miso broth. Add the chashu pork slices, spicy prawns, enoki mushrooms and bamboo shoots. Sprinkle over the sesame seeds and shio kombu to garnish and serve straight away.

NOTES

Shio kombu is a seaweed garnish available from most Japanese grocery stores. La doubanjiang can be purchased from most Asian supermarkets.

SEAFOOD MISO RAMEN

SERVES 2

3 teaspoons peanut oil

1 garlic clove, smashed

1 teaspoon finely grated ginger

1 tablespoon Dashi Stock (see page 19) or water

12 mussels, cleaned and debearded

6 raw prawns (shrimp), shelled and deveined

6 scallops, with roe attached

800 ml (27 fl oz) Miso Broth (see page 14), simmering

2 portions thick Ramen Noodles (see page 20), cooked al dente and drained

20 g (¾ oz) fresh wood ear mushrooms, sliced

4 slices Narutomaki (see page 34) *fish cake*

1 nori sheet, cut into quarters

2 Seaweed Butter Bombs (see page 39)

2 tablespoons thinly shaved bonito flakes (hanakatsuo)

Heat 2 teaspoons of the oil in a wok over medium — high heat. Add the garlic and ginger and stir-fry for 1 — 2 minutes. Add the dashi stock or water and the mussels, then cover with a lid. Increase the heat to high and steam for 2 — 3 minutes, until the mussels have opened. Remove the pan from the heat and set aside.

Preheat a grill (broiler) to medium — high.

Place the prawns and scallops in a bowl and toss through the remaining oil to coat. Grill the prawns for 2 — 3 minutes and the scallops for 1 — 2 minutes, turning halfway, until just cooked through.

Add the cooked mussels and their residual liquid to the simmering miso broth.

To assemble the ramen, quickly and evenly divide the warm drained noodles between two bowls and pour over the hot miso broth and mussels. Add the prawns, scallops, mushrooms, narutomaki, nori and butter bombs. Finish with a sprinkling of shaved bonito flakes.

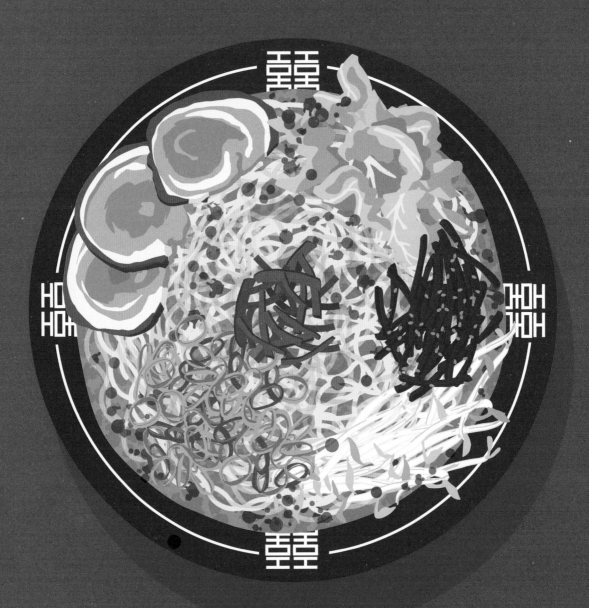

CHASHU PORK, CABBAGE AND BEAN SHOOT MISO RAMEN

SERVES 2

1 teaspoon peanut oil

1 teaspoon toasted sesame oil

1 garlic clove, finely grated

1 spring onion (scallion), finely sliced

120 g (4½ oz) shredded cabbage

50 g (1¾ oz) bean sprouts

6 slices Chashu Pork (see page 28)

800 ml (27 fl oz) Miso Broth (see page 14), simmering

2 portions thick Ramen Noodles (see page 20), cooked al dente and drained

20 g pickled ginger (beni shoga)

chilli oil, for drizzling

Tsukudani (see page 38), to serve

Heat the oils in a wok over high heat and quickly stir-fry the garlic, spring onion, cabbage and bean sprouts for 1 — 2 minutes.

Place the chashu slices into the simmering broth to gently warm, or warm through in the chashu braising liquid.

To assemble the ramen, quickly and evenly divide the warm drained noodles between two bowls and pour over the hot miso broth. Add the chashu pork, stir-fried vegetables and pickled ginger, and finish with a drizzle of chilli oil. Serve with tsukudani on the side.

BARBECUE CHICKEN MISO RAMEN

SERVES 2

2 portions thick Ramen Noodles (see page 20), cooked al dente and drained

100 g (3½ oz) finely shredded Chinese broccoli

265 g (9½ oz/1½ cups) shredded store-bought barbecued chicken

800 ml (27 fl oz) Miso Broth (see page 14), simmering

2 Ajitsuke Tamago (see page 26), halved

100 g (3½ oz) fresh corn kernels, blanched

2 teaspoons cold butter

2 teaspoons Japanese chilli seasoning (*shichimi togarashi*) (see note)

Furikake (see page 37), for garnish

To assemble the ramen, quickly and evenly divide the warm drained noodles between two bowls and add the Chinese broccoli and barbecued chicken. Pour over the hot miso broth and add the ajitsuke tamago and corn. Dot the corn with butter, sprinkle over the chilli seasoning and garnish with furikake.

NOTE

Shichimi togarashi can be purchased from most Asian supermarkets.

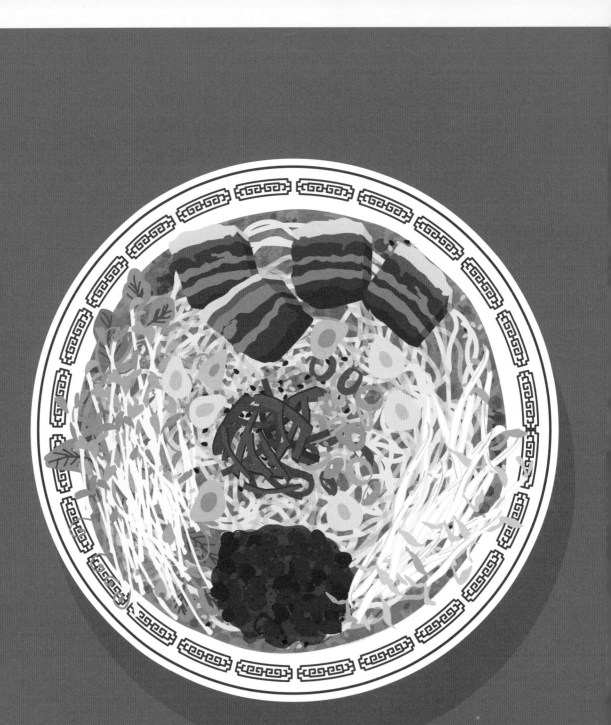

KAKUNI MISO RAMEN

SERVES 2

3 teaspoons peanut oil

1 garlic clove, finely grated

50 g (1¾ oz) snow pea (mangetout) shoots

50 g (1¾ oz) bean sprouts

pinch of caster (superfine) sugar

pinch of sea salt

1 teaspoon Chinese rice wine

1 teaspoon toasted sesame oil

2 portions thick Ramen Noodles (see page 20), cooked al dente and drained

800 ml (27 fl oz) Miso Broth (see page 14), simmering

8 — 10 pieces of Kakuni (see page 30), warmed *pork belly*

2 teaspoons spicy chilli bean paste (la doubanjiang), or to taste (see note)

20 g (¾ oz) pickled ginger (beni shoga)

Garlic Chips (see page 36), for garnish

Heat the peanut oil in a wok over medium — low heat, add the garlic and slowly fry, taking care not to burn the garlic. Add the snow pea shoots and bean sprouts, increase the heat to medium and toss the wok to combine. Add the sugar, salt, rice wine and sesame oil, toss for 1 — 2 minutes, then remove from the heat.

To assemble the ramen, quickly and evenly divide the warm drained noodles between two bowls and pour over the hot miso broth. Add the stir-fried vegetables, kakuni, spicy chilli bean paste and pickled ginger. Sprinkle over the garlic chips and serve.

NOTE

La doubanjiang *can be purchased from most Asian supermarkets.*

SMOKED TOFU, MISO-GLAZED CARROTS AND EGGPLANT MISO RAMEN

SERVES 2

2 tablespoons white miso paste

2 tablespoons mirin

1 tablespoon sake

1 teaspoon caster (superfine) sugar

1½ tablespoons peanut oil

2 teaspoons toasted sesame oil

150 g (5½ oz) Japanese eggplant (aubergine), cut into 3 cm (1¼ in) cubes

120 g (4½ oz) carrot, julienned

2 portions thick Ramen Noodles (see page 20), cooked al dente and drained

800 ml (27 fl oz) Vegan Broth (see page 18), simmering

200 g (7 oz) smoked tofu, cut into 6 slices

50 g (1¾ oz) bean sprouts

2 teaspoons toasted sesame seeds

chilli oil, for drizzling

Umami Mushroom Powder (see page 40), for garnish

In a small bowl, whisk together the miso paste, mirin, sake and sugar.

Heat the oils in a wok over medium — high heat. Add the eggplant and stir-fry for about 2 minutes, then add the carrot and stir-fry for a further 1 minute. Add the miso mixture and stir-fry for another minute.

To assemble the ramen, quickly and evenly divide the warm drained noodles between two bowls and pour over the hot vegan broth. Add the vegetables, smoked tofu, bean sprouts and sesame seeds. Drizzle over the chilli oil and garnish with umami mushroom powder.

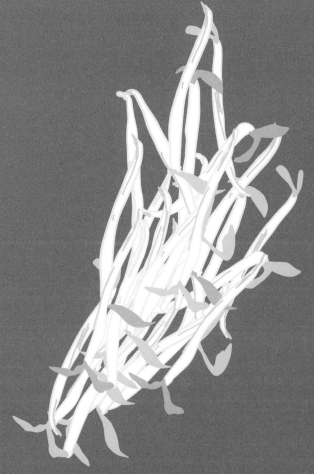

SHOYU RAMEN

PORK KARAAGE SHOYU RAMEN

SERVES 2

seaweed

2 teaspoons dried wakame

2 portions thin Ramen Noodles (see page 20), cooked al dente and drained

800 ml (27 fl oz) Shoyu Broth (see page 15), simmering

Fish cakes

2 Narutomaki slices (see page 34)

20 g (¾ oz) enoki mushrooms

1 Ajitsuke Tamago (see page 26), halved

seasoned egg

2 spring onions (scallions), thinly sliced

Japanese Quick Pickles (see page 38), to serve

PORK KARAAGE

2 garlic cloves, finely grated

10 g (¼ oz) ginger, finely grated

1 tablespoon soy sauce

1½ tablespoons sake

2 teaspoons toasted sesame oil

300 g (10½ oz) pork loin, cut into 4 cm (1½ in) pieces

peanut oil, for deep-frying

80 g (2¾ oz/½ cup) potato starch

¼ teaspoon sea salt

¼ teaspoon ground white pepper

Rinse the wakame and rehydrate in a bowl of cold water. Drain well.

To make the pork karaage, combine the garlic, ginger, soy sauce, sake and sesame oil in a bowl. Add the pork, stir to coat, then cover and refrigerate for 30 minutes.

Heat enough oil for deep-frying in a deep-fryer or wok to 190°C (375°F).

Combine the potato starch, salt and pepper in a bowl.

Remove the pork from the fridge, drain and discard the marinade.

Toss the pork through the potato starch, coating thoroughly. Fry the pork in batches for 3 — 4 minutes until cooked through. Drain on a wire rack.

To assemble the ramen, quickly and evenly divide the warm drained noodles between two bowls and pour over the hot shoyu broth. Add the wakame, narutomaki, enoki mushrooms, ajitsuke tamago and spring onion. Top with the pork karaage and serve with Japanese pickles on the side.

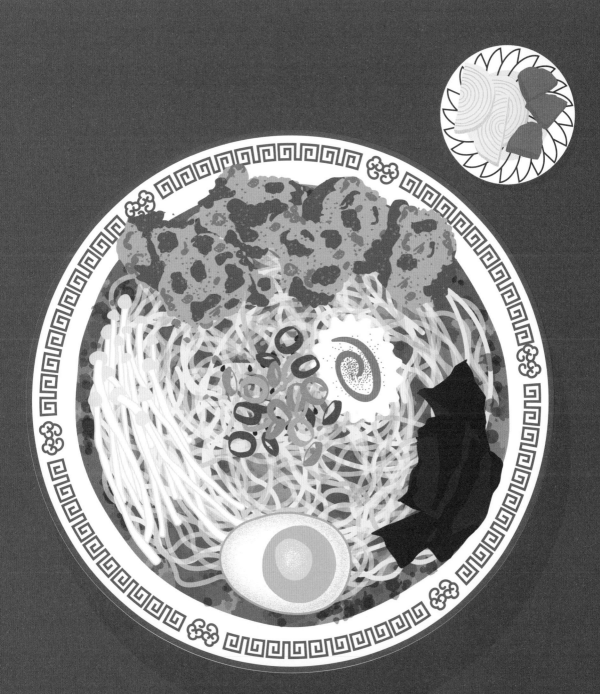

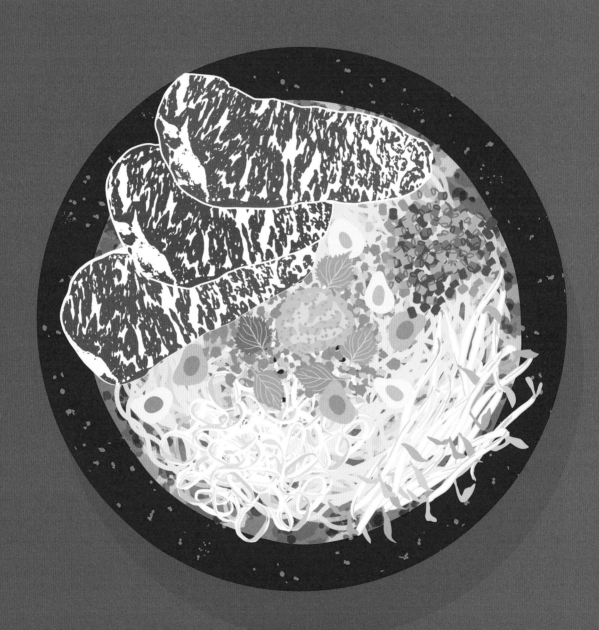

WAGYU SHOYU RAMEN

SERVES 2

50 — 60 g (1¾ — 2 oz) fresh
wagyu sirloin

peanut oil, for deep-frying

60 g (2 oz) leek, white part only,
sliced

2 portions thin Ramen Noodles (see
page 20), cooked al dente
and drained

800 ml (27 fl oz) Shoyu Broth
(see page 15), simmering

40 g (1½ oz) bean sprouts

2 tablespoons roasted peanuts,
chopped

2 teaspoons thinly sliced garlic chives

2 tablespoons shio micro herbs
(see note)

freshly grated wasabi (see note),
to taste

Garlic Chips (see page 36),
for garnish

Tightly wrap the wagyu in plastic wrap and freeze for 1 — 2 hours
until semi frozen.

Remove the plastic wrap and slice the wagyu across the grain as
thinly as possible into 2 — 3 mm (⅛ in) thick slices, carpaccio style.
Set aside.

Heat enough oil for deep-frying in a deep-fryer or wok to 175°C
(340°F). Add the leek and fry until golden brown and crisp. Drain
on paper towels.

To assemble the ramen, quickly and evenly divide the warm
drained noodles between two bowls and pour over the hot
shoyu broth. Add the sliced wagyu, leek, bean sprouts, peanuts
and garlic chives. Top with the shio micro herbs, a grating of fresh
wasabi and garnish with garlic chips.

NOTE
*Shio micro herbs and fresh wasabi can be found at most Asian supermarkets.
Substitute small shio leaves and fresh horseradish, if unavailable.*

BEAN CURD, ZUCCHINI AND KIMCHI VEGAN SHOYU RAMEN

SERVES 2

2 bean curd strands (see note)

800 ml (27 fl oz) Vegan Broth (see page 18) made with Shoyu Tare (see page 15), simmering

2 portions thick Ramen Noodles (see page 20), cooked al dente and drained

100 g (3½ oz) zucchini (courgette), shredded or spiralised

100 g (3½ oz) Kimchi (see page 35)

2 tablespoons kimchi juice (optional)

100 g (3½ oz) fresh corn kernels, blanched

2 teaspoons toasted sesame oil

mizuna leaves (Japanese mustard greens), for garnish

Wakame Gomasio (see page 36), for garnish

Place the bean curd strands in a heatproof bowl, pour over boiling water to cover and soak for 1 hour until rehydrated. Rinse, drain and cut into 3 cm (1¼ in) lengths. Add to the simmering vegan broth.

To assemble the ramen, quickly and evenly divide the warm drained noodles between two bowls. Pour over the hot broth along with the bean curd strands. Add the zucchini, kimchi, kimchi juice, if using, and corn. Drizzle over the sesame oil and garnish with mizuna leaves and wakame gomasio.

NOTE
Bean curd strands are also called bean curd sticks. They can be purchased at most Asian supermarkets.

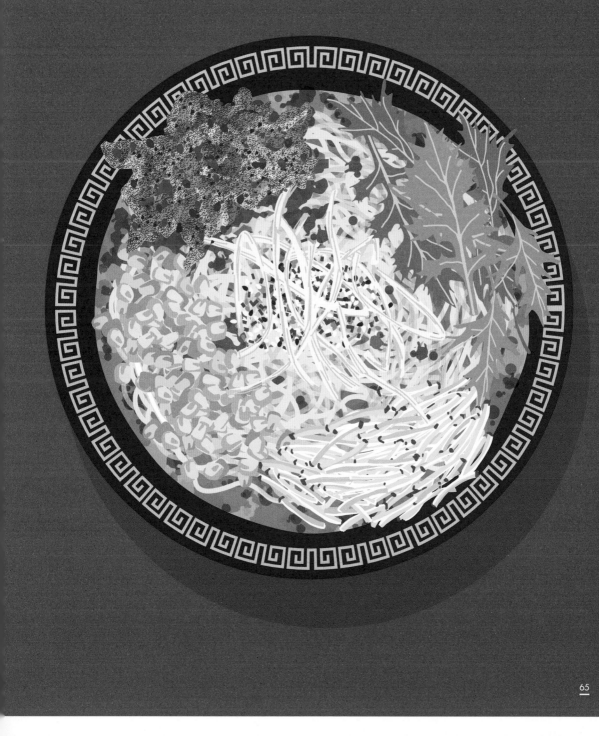

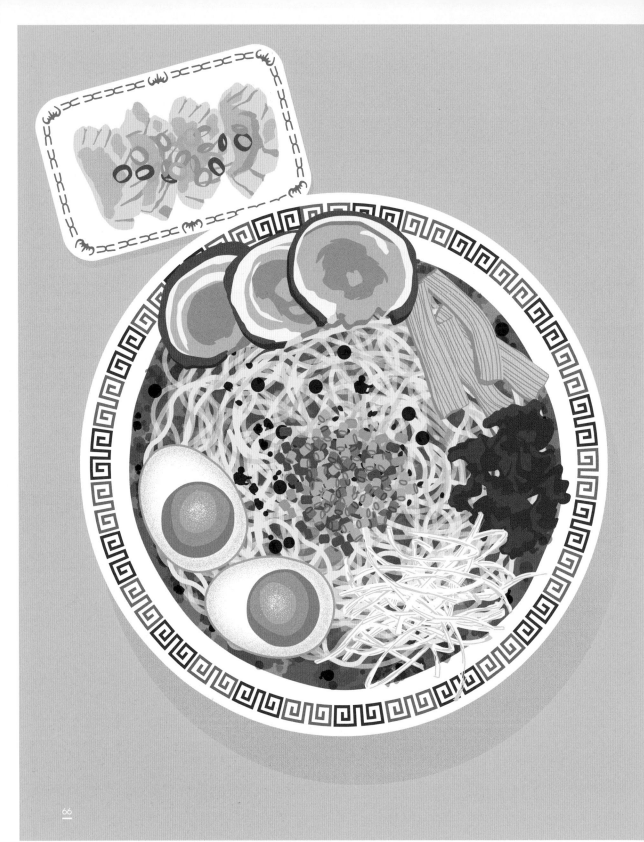

SEAFOOD GYOZA AND
CHASHU SHOYU RAMEN

SERVES 2

6 slices Chashu Pork (see page 28)

800 ml (27 fl oz) Shoyu Broth (see page 15), simmering

2 portions thin Ramen Noodles (see page 20), cooked al dente and drained

20 g (¾ oz) fresh wood ear mushrooms, thinly sliced

8 pieces fermented bamboo shoots (menma)

60 g (2 oz) leek, white part only, julienned

1 Ajitsuke Tamago (see page 26), halved

1 tablespoon finely chopped chives

Black Mayu (see page 40), for drizzling (optional)

6 cooked Seafood Gyoza (see page 32)

Warm the chashu slices in the simmering shoyu broth.

To assemble the ramen, quickly and evenly divide the warm drained noodles between two bowls and pour over the hot shoyu broth along with the chashu slices. Add the mushrooms, bamboo shoots, leek and ajitsuke tamago. Top with the chives and drizzle over a little black mayu, if using. Serve with the seafood gyoza on the side.

MUSHROOM SHOYU RAMEN

SERVES 2

25 g (1 oz) butter or oil

1 teaspoon toasted sesame oil

2 garlic cloves, chopped

2 spring onions (scallions), sliced

400 g (14 oz) mixed mushrooms, such as shiitake, enoki, wood ear, king brown and shimeji, sliced

2 portions thick Ramen Noodles (see page 20), cooked al dente and drained

800 ml (27 fl oz) Vegan Broth (see page 18) made with Shoyu Tare (see page 15), simmering

1 nori sheet, cut into quarters

1 tablespoon toasted sesame seeds

½ teaspoon lemon zest, for garnish

Umami Mushroom Powder (see page 40), for garnish

Heat the butter or oil, sesame oil and garlic in a wok over medium — high heat and sauté until fragrant. Add the spring onion and mushrooms, and sauté for a further 2 — 3 minutes until golden brown.

To assemble the ramen, quickly and evenly divide the warm drained noodles between two bowls and pour over the hot broth. Add the stir-fried mushroom mixture and nori. Sprinkle over the sesame seeds and garnish with the lemon zest and umami mushroom powder.

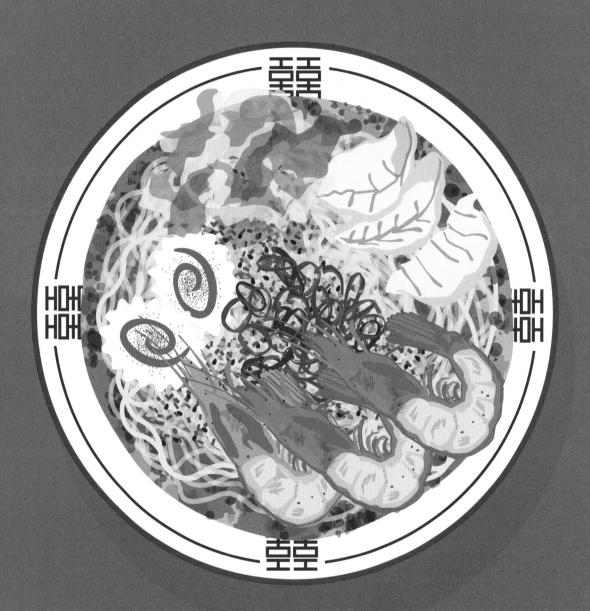

SEAFOOD GYOZA AND GRILLED PRAWN SHOYU RAMEN

SERVES 2

6 large raw prawns (shrimp), shells on

1 teaspoon toasted sesame oil

2 garlic cloves, finely grated

2 teaspoons finely sliced red chilli

2 portions thick Ramen Noodles (see page 20), cooked al dente and drained

800 ml (27 fl oz) Shoyu Broth (see page 15), simmering

6 cooked Seafood Gyoza (see page 32)

4 slices Narutomaki (see page 34)

2 teaspoons Furikake (see page 37)

½ teaspoon bonito flakes (*katsuobushi*)

ponzu, for drizzling

Use a sharp knife to butterfly the prawns from their middle to the tail, open up and devein. Transfer to a small bowl and combine with the oil, garlic and chilli. Heat a griddle pan over high heat and cook the prawns for 1 minute on each side or until cooked through.

To assemble the ramen, quickly and evenly divide the warm drained noodles between two bowls and pour over the hot shoyu broth. Add the prawns, gyoza and narutomaki. Sprinkle over the furikake and bonito flakes and finish with a drizzle of ponzu.

KAKUNI, VEGETABLE GYOZA AND
QUAIL EGG SHOYU RAMEN

SERVES 2

4 quail eggs

pork belly

6 — 8 pieces Kakuni (see page 30)

800 ml (27 fl oz) Shoyu Broth (see page 15), simmering

2 portions thick Ramen Noodles (see page 20), cooked al dente and drained

6 cooked Vegetable Gyoza (see page 31)

40 g (1½ oz) bean sprouts

2 spring onions (scallions), thinly sliced

pickled ginger (*beni shoga*), to serve

Pickled Shiitake Mushrooms (see page 37), to serve

Bring a saucepan of water to the boil, add the quail eggs and cook for 2½ minutes. Cool in an ice bath for 3 minutes to stop the cooking process, then peel and cut in half.

Add the kakuni to the shoyu broth to warm through.

To assemble the ramen, quickly and evenly divide the drained noodles between two bowls and pour over the hot shoyu broth along with the kakuni. Add the gyoza, bean sprouts, spring onion and top with the egg. Serve with pickled ginger and pickled mushrooms on the side.

TONKOTSU RAMEN

CHICKEN KARAAGE TONKOTSU RAMEN

SERVES 2

2 boneless chicken thighs, skin on, cut into 5 cm (2 in) pieces

80 g (2¾ oz/½ cup) potato starch

¼ teaspoon sea salt

¼ teaspoon black pepper

peanut oil, for deep-frying

2 portions thin Ramen Noodles (see page 20), cooked al dente and drained

800 ml (27 fl oz) Tonkotsu Broth (see page 16), simmering

2 Ajitsuke Tamago (see page 26), halved

2 spring onions (scallions), thinly sliced

2 teaspoons toasted sesame seeds

Japanese chilli seasoning (*shichimi togarashi*), for garnish (see note)

MARINADE

2 garlic cloves, finely grated

10 g (¼ oz) ginger, finely grated

1½ tablespoons soy sauce

1½ tablespoons sweet sake

1 teaspoon toasted sesame oil

¼ teaspoon ground white pepper

¼ teaspoon Japanese chilli seasoning (*shichimi togarashi*)

To make the karaage chicken, combine the marinade ingredients in a large bowl, add the chicken and mix well to combine. Cover with plastic wrap and refrigerate for 30 minutes.

Combine the potato starch, salt and pepper in a bowl.

Drain the chicken, discarding the marinade, and toss through the seasoned potato starch, coating the chicken completely.

Heat enough peanut oil for deep-frying in a deep-fryer or large saucepan to 170°C (340°F). Fry the chicken in batches for 3 minutes, then transfer to wire racks to drain. Increase the temperature to 190°C (380°F) and fry the chicken again for 30 — 60 seconds until golden brown and cooked through.

To assemble the ramen, quickly and evenly divide the warm drained noodles between two bowls and pour over the hot tonkotsu broth. Top with the ajitsuke tamago, spring onion and sesame seeds. Serve with the karaage on the side for dipping into the broth and garnish with the *shichimi togarashi*.

NOTE

Shichimi togarashi *is available from most Asian supermarkets.*

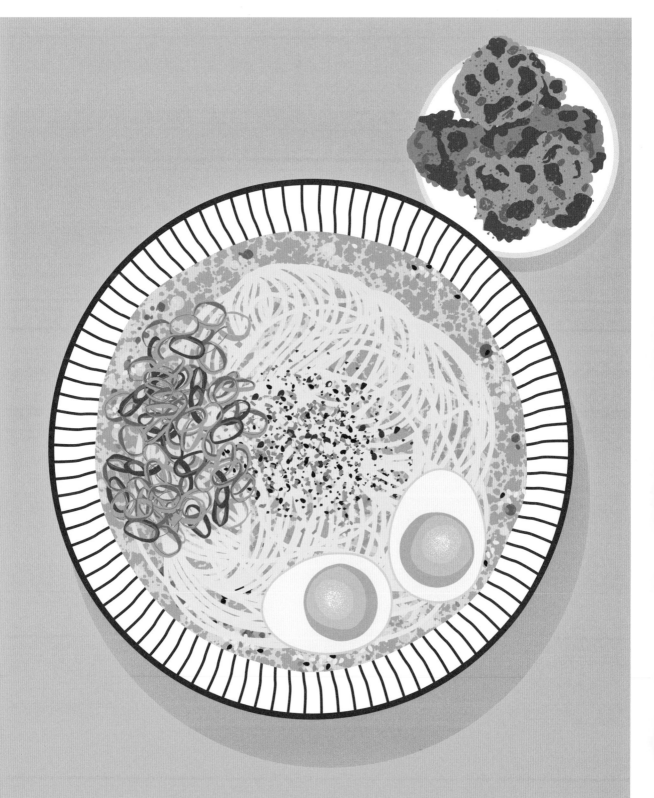

PORK SHOULDER, ONSEN TAMAGO AND NARUTOMAKI TONKOTSU RAMEN

SERVES 2

1½ tablespoons dried wakame

1 tablespoon Rendered Pork Fat (see page 41)

200 g (7 oz) Shredded Pork Shoulder (see page 29)

2 teaspoons soy sauce

2 teaspoons mirin

2 portions thin Ramen Noodles (see page 20), cooked al dente and drained

800 ml (27 fl oz) Tonkotsu Broth (see page 16), simmering

4 slices Narutomaki (see page 34)

2 spring onions (scallions), thinly sliced

2 teaspoons toasted black sesame seeds

2 Onsen Tamago (see page 27)

Rinse the wakame and rehydrate in a bowl of cold water. Drain well.

Place the pork fat in a frying pan over medium — high heat, add the shredded pork and cook for 1 — 2 minutes. Add the soy sauce and mirin, and toss through. Continue cooking until the pork is sticky and crisp.

To assemble the ramen, quickly and evenly divide the warm drained noodles between two bowls and pour over the hot tonkotsu broth. Top with the narutomaki, spring onion, wakame and shredded pork. Sprinkle over the toasted black sesame seeds and serve with the onsen tamago on the side.

CHASHU, AJITSUKE TAMAGO AND
MENMA TONKOTSU RAMEN

SERVES 2

6 slices Chashu Pork (see page 28)

2 teaspoons Rendered Pork Fat (see page 41)

2 portions thin Ramen Noodles (see page 20), cooked al dente and drained

800 ml (27 fl oz) Tonkotsu Broth (see page 16), simmering

20 g (¾ oz) fresh wood ear mushrooms, sliced

8 pieces fermented bamboo shoots (*menma*)

1 tablespoon Wakame Gomasio (see page 36)

2 Ajitsuke Tamago (see page 26), halved

1 nori sheet, cut into quarters

Black Mayu (see page 40), for drizzling

2 teaspoons thinly sliced garlic chives

Cook the chashu slices and pork fat in a large frying pan over medium heat until warm and melting.

To assemble the ramen, quickly and evenly divide the warm drained noodles between two bowls and pour over the hot tonkotsu broth. Top with the wood ear mushrooms, bamboo shoots, ajitsuke tamago, nori pieces and chashu slices. Drizzle over the remaining pork fat from the frying pan and a little black mayu. Finish with a sprinkle of garlic chives.

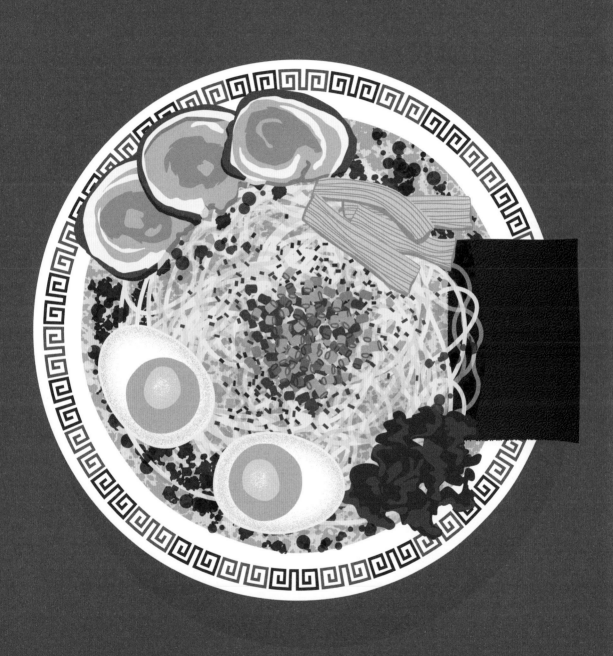

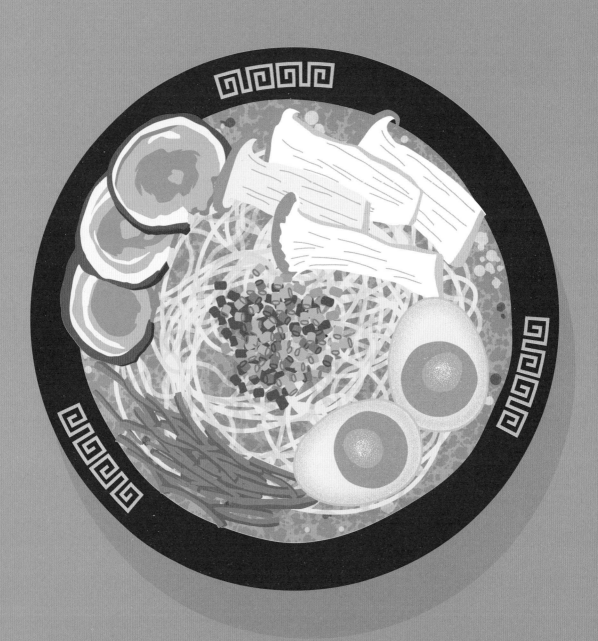

CHASHU PORK AND KING OYSTER MUSHROOM TONKOTSU RAMEN

SERVES 2

20 g (¾ oz) butter

1 garlic clove, thinly sliced

100 g (3½ oz) king oyster mushrooms, sliced

sea salt and black pepper

2 teaspoons soy sauce

1 tablespoon Rendered Pork Fat (see page 41)

6 slices Chashu Pork (see page 28)

2 portions thin Ramen Noodles (see page 20), cooked al dente and drained

800 ml (27 fl oz) Tonkotsu Broth (see page 16), simmering

2 Ajitsuke Tamago (see page 26), halved

1 medium-sized carrot, julienned

1 tablespoon chopped chives

1 tablespoon warmed chashu cooking liquid (see page 28), for drizzling (optional)

Melt the butter in a wok or frying pan over medium — high heat. Add the garlic and mushrooms and season with salt and pepper. Cook, stirring, for 2 — 3 minutes. Add the soy sauce and cook for a further 1 minute until the mushrooms are golden brown, then remove and set aside.

Melt the pork fat in the same pan, add the chashu slices and warm through until meltingly tender.

To assemble the ramen, quickly and evenly divide the warm drained noodles between two bowls and pour over the hot tonkotsu broth. Add the mushrooms, chashu slices, ajitsuke tamago, carrot and chives. Drizzle over the remaining pork fat from the frying pan and the warmed chashu cooking liquid, if using.

SPICY GROUND PORK
TONKOTSU RAMEN

SERVES 2

1 tablespoon peanut oil

300 g (10½ oz) minced (ground) pork

¼ teaspoon ground white pepper

1 tablespoon mirin

2 teaspoons caster (superfine) sugar

1 tablespoon soy sauce

1 tablespoon spicy chilli bean paste (la doubanjiang), or to taste (see notes)

2 teaspoons finely grated ginger

1 spring onion (scallion), thinly sliced

2 portions thin Ramen Noodles, cooked al dente and drained (see page 20)

800 ml (27 fl oz) Tonkotsu Broth (see page 16), simmering

6 cooked Pork Gyoza (see page 33)

10 green beans, thinly sliced into rounds

dried chilli threads, for garnish (see notes)

2 Onsen Tamago (see page 27)

Heat the oil in a wok over medium — high heat and add the minced pork. Stir-fry for 2 — 3 minutes, breaking up the meat with a wooden spoon. Add the white pepper, mirin, sugar, soy sauce, spicy chilli bean paste and ginger, and cook for a further 1 — 2 minutes. Toss through the spring onion and set aside.

To assemble the ramen, quickly and evenly divide the warm drained noodles between two bowls and pour over the hot tonkotsu broth. Add the fried pork mixture and top with the pork gyoza and green beans. Garnish with dried chilli threads and serve with the onsen tamago on the side.

NOTES

La doubanjiang can be purchased from most Asian supermarkets.
Dried chilli threads are also known as Korean chilli threads, silgochu or chilli strings. They can be purchased from most Asian supermarkets.

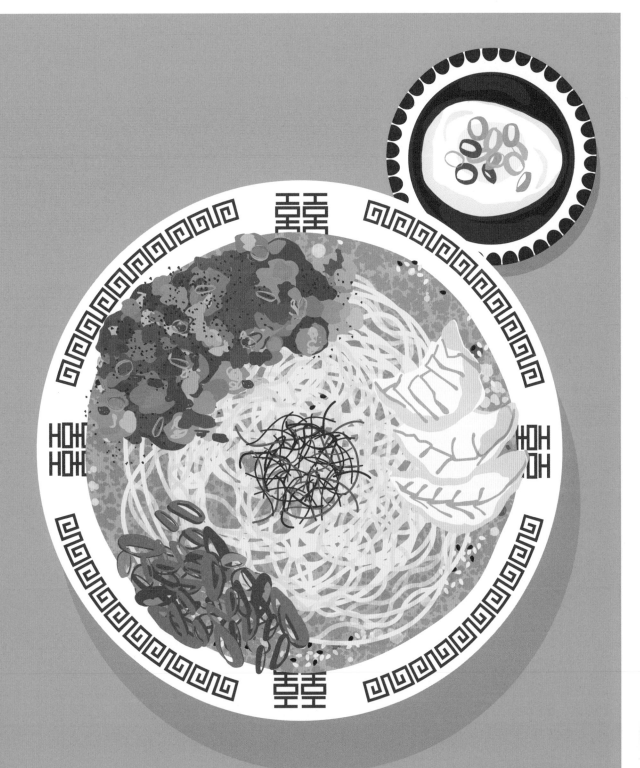

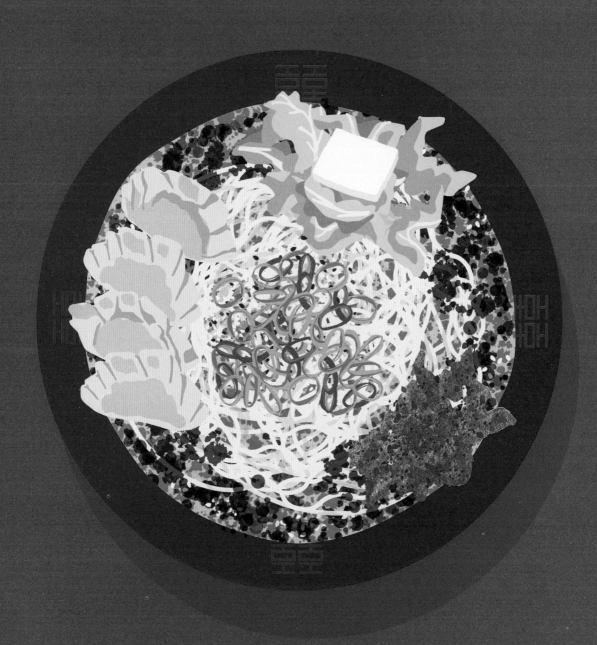

PORK GYOZA AND BUTTERED CABBAGE TONKOTSU RAMEN

SERVES 2

60 g (2 oz) shredded cabbage

15 g (½ oz) butter

cracked black pepper

2 portions thin Ramen Noodles (see page 20), cooked al dente and drained

800 ml (27 fl oz) Tonkotsu Broth (see page 16), simmering

8 cooked Pork Gyoza (see page 33)

100 g (3½ oz) Kimchi (see page 35)

1 tablespoon kimchi juice (optional)

2 spring onions (scallions), thinly sliced

Black Mayu (see page 40), for drizzling

Bring a large saucepan of water to the boil over medium — high heat. Add the cabbage and blanch for 1 — 1½ minutes. Strain the cabbage into a heatproof bowl, toss with the butter and season with pepper.

To assemble the ramen, quickly and evenly divide the warm drained noodles between two bowls and pour over the hot tonkotsu broth. Add the pork gyoza, cabbage, kimchi, kimchi juice, if using, and spring onion. Drizzle over a little black mayu and serve straight away.

SALT AND PEPPER TOFU
TONKOTSU RAMEN

SERVES 2

2 portions thin Ramen Noodles (see page 20), cooked al dente and drained

800 ml (27 fl oz) Tonkotsu Broth (see page 16), simmering

50 g (1¾ oz) mizuna leaves (Japanese mustard greens)

2 Ajitsuke Tamago (see page 26), halved

2 teaspoons black sesame seeds

black tahini, for drizzling (see note)

SALT AND PEPPER TOFU

40 g (1½ oz) cornflour (corn starch)

3 teaspoons sea salt

½ teaspoon chilli flakes

1 teaspoon cracked black pepper

1 teaspoon ground white pepper

1 teaspoon toasted and ground Sichuan peppercorns

250 g (9 oz) firm tofu, drained, cut into 3 cm x 2.5 cm (1¼ in x 1 in) pieces

peanut oil, for deep-frying

1 teaspoon toasted sesame oil

3 red chillies, thinly sliced

2 garlic cloves, finely grated

1 tablespoon finely grated ginger

1 spring onion (scallion), thinly sliced

2 tablespoons soy sauce

1 tablespoon caster (superfine) sugar

To make the salt and pepper tofu, combine the cornflour, salt, chilli flakes and peppers in a large bowl. Add the tofu and toss to coat.

Heat enough oil for deep-frying in a deep-fryer, large saucepan or wok to 185°C (365°F). Working in batches, deep-fry the tofu for 1 — 2 minutes, then transfer to a wire rack to drain.

Heat 1 tablespoon of peanut oil in a wok over medium — high heat and add the sesame oil, chilli and garlic. Cook, stirring, for 30 — 40 seconds, then add the ginger, spring onion, soy sauce and sugar. Cook for a further 30 — 40 seconds, then toss through the tofu to coat.

To assemble the ramen, quickly and evenly divide the warm drained noodles between two bowls and pour over the hot tonkotsu broth. Add the tofu, mizuna leaves and adjitsuke tamago, and sprinkle over the sesame seeds. Drizzle over a little black tahini and serve straight away.

NOTE

Black tahini can be purchased from most Asian supermarkets or health-food stores.

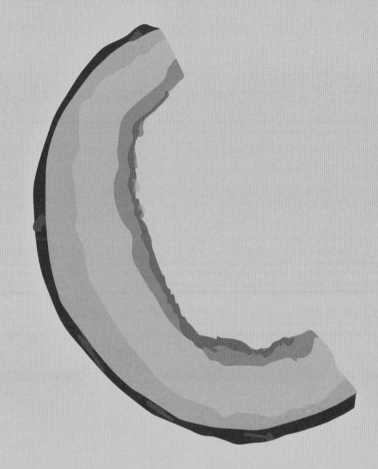

SHIO RAMEN

ROASTED SCALLOPS, BUTTERED CORN AND LEEK SHIO RAMEN

SERVES 2

1 leek, white part only, sliced into 1 cm (½ in) rounds

800 ml (27 fl oz) Shio Broth (see page 17), simmering

2 tablespoons peanut oil

12 scallops, with roe attached

sea salt and ground white pepper

2 tablespoons melted butter

2 portions thick Ramen Noodles (see page 20), cooked al dente and drained

100 g (3½ oz) fresh corn kernels, blanched

2 Seaweed Butter Bombs (see page 39)

dried chilli threads, for garnish (see note)

Add the leeks to the simmering shio broth to cook through.

Heat the oil in a frying pan over medium—high heat. Season the scallops with salt and pepper, then cook, in batches, for 1—1½ minutes. Flip them over, drizzle each scallop with a little melted butter and cook for a further 30—40 seconds until golden brown.

To assemble the ramen, quickly and evenly divide the drained noodles between two bowls and pour over the hot shio broth along with the leek. Add the scallops and corn, and top with the seaweed butter bombs. Garnish with chilli threads and serve straight away.

<u>NOTE</u>

Dried chilli threads are also known as Korean chilli threads, silgochu or chilli strings. They can be purchased from most Asian supermarkets.

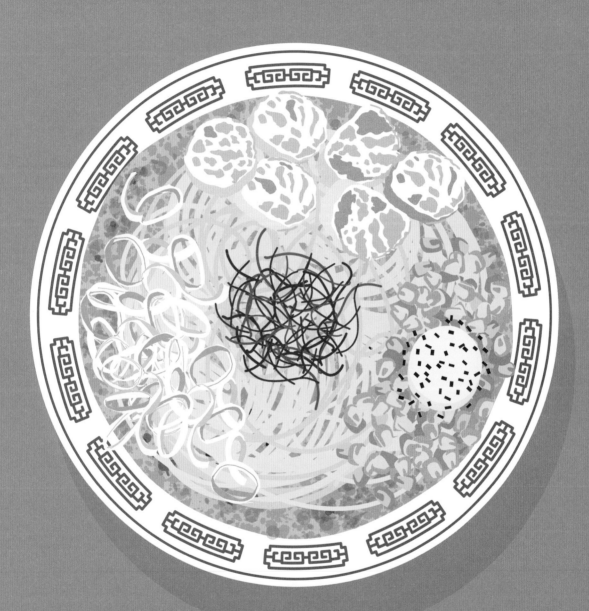

PANKO CHICKEN SHIO RAMEN

SERVES 2

2 x 150 g (5½ oz) chicken breasts, pounded until 1 cm (½ in) thick

sea salt and freshly cracked black pepper

50 g (1¾ oz/⅓ cup) plain (all-purpose) flour

1 egg, beaten

60 g (2 oz/1 cup) panko breadcrumbs

peanut oil, for shallow-frying

2 portions thick Ramen Noodles (see page 20), cooked al dente and drained

800 ml (27 fl oz) Shio Broth (see page 17), simmering

8 slices fermented bamboo shoots (menma)

100 g (3½ oz) spinach, blanched and squeezed dry

2 spring onions (scallions), thinly sliced

tonkatsu sauce, for drizzling (optional) (see note)

2 Onsen Tamago (see page 27)

Season the chicken with salt and pepper. Place the flour in a shallow bowl, the beaten egg in a second bowl and the breadcrumbs in a third. Dredge the chicken in the flour and shake off the excess. Dip into the egg, then coat in the breadcrumbs.

Heat 3 cm (1¼ in) oil in a wok to 190°C (375°F). Fry the chicken for 2 — 3 minutes on each side until golden brown and cooked through.

To assemble the ramen, quickly and evenly divide the drained noodles between two bowls and pour over the hot shio broth. Slice the chicken into 5 — 6 slices each and lay on top of the noodles. Add the bamboo shoots, spinach and spring onion. Finish with a drizzle of tonkatsu sauce over the chicken, if using, and serve with the onsen tamago on the side.

NOTE

Tonkatsu sauce can be purchased from most Asian supermarkets.

SPINACH, BOK CHOY AND EDAMAME SHIO RAMEN

SERVES 2

1½ tablespoons dried wakame

2 portions thin Ramen Noodles (see page 20), cooked al dente and drained

800 ml (27 fl oz) Shio Broth (see page 17), simmering

100 g (3½ oz) baby spinach, blanched
and squeezed dry

1 baby bok choy, halved and blanched

95 g (3¼ oz/⅔ cup) edamame, blanched

2 Ajitsuke Tamago (see page 26), halved

3 teaspoons Wakame Gomasio (see page 36)

garlic chives, for garnish

toasted sesame oil, for drizzling

Rinse the wakame and rehydrate in a bowl of cold water. Drain well.

To assemble the ramen, quickly and evenly divide the drained noodles between two bowls and pour over the hot shio broth. Add the wakame, the blanched vegetables and ajitsuke tamago. Sprinkle over the wakame gomasio and garnish with the chives. Finish with a drizzle of sesame oil.

SQUID INK SHIO RAMEN

SERVES 2

2 teaspoons peanut oil

250 g (9 oz) squid tubes, cleaned and cut into 1 cm (½ in) thick slices

2 teaspoons ponzu

2 portions thin Ramen Noodles (see page 20), cooked al dente and drained

2 teaspoons squid ink (see note)

800 ml (27 fl oz) Shio Broth (see page 17), simmering

4 slices Narutomaki (see page 34)

small handful watercress

3 teaspoons salmon roe

freshly cracked black pepper

toasted black sesame seeds, for garnish

Heat the oil in a wok over medium — high heat. Add the squid and quickly stir-fry for about 1 minute until opaque and just cooked through. Add the ponzu and toss to coat. Remove from the heat.

To assemble the ramen, quickly and evenly divide the drained noodles between two bowls. Quickly whisk the squid ink into the simmering broth, then pour over the noodles. Add the squid, narutomaki, watercress and salmon roe. Garnish with cracked black pepper and a few sesame seeds.

NOTE
Squid ink is available in sachets from gourmet food stores and delicatessens.

KAKUNI, FRIED EGG AND SPRING ONION SHIO RAMEN

SERVES 2

1 tablespoon chicken fat, Rendered Pork Fat (see page 41) or peanut oil

2 eggs

800 ml (27 fl oz) Shio Broth (see page 17), simmering

2 portions thick Ramen Noodles (see page 20), cooked al dente and drained

8 — 10 pieces Kakuni (see page 30)

8 pieces fermented bamboo shoots (menma)

2 spring onions (scallions), thinly sliced

sliced red chilli, for garnish

chilli oil, for drizzling (optional)

Pickled Shiitake Mushrooms (see page 37), to serve

Heat the fat or oil in a frying pan over medium — high heat, crack in the eggs and fry until the bottoms and edges are crisp and the yolk is cooked to your liking.

To assemble the ramen, quickly and evenly divide the drained noodles between two bowls and pour over the hot shio broth. Add the kakuni, bamboo shoots, eggs and spring onion. Garnish with a little sliced red chilli and drizzle over some chilli oil, if you like. Serve with pickled shiitake mushrooms on the side.

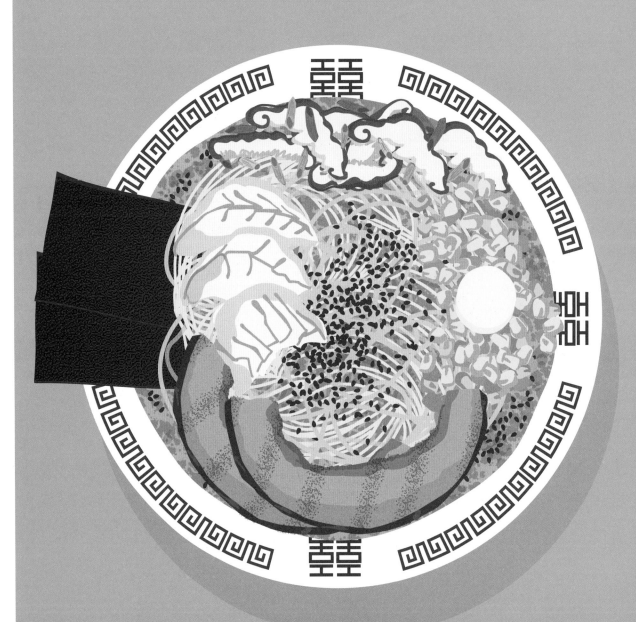

VEGETABLE GYOZA, KABOCHA AND SHIITAKE SHIO RAMEN

SERVES 2

4 x 1 cm (½ in) thick wedges kabocha (Japanese pumpkin)

2 teaspoons butter

2 teaspoons toasted sesame oil

1 garlic clove, finely grated

4 fresh shiitake mushrooms, sliced

1 spring onion (scallion), cut into 2 cm (¾ in) lengths

1 teaspoon soy sauce

2 portions thin Ramen Noodles (see page 20), cooked al dente and drained

800 ml (27 fl oz) Shio Broth (see page 17), simmering

6 cooked Vegetable Gyoza (see page 31)

1 nori sheet, cut into quarters

100 g (3½ oz) fresh corn kernels, blanched

2 Miso Butter Bombs (see page 39)

2 teaspoons toasted black sesame seeds

Umami Mushroom Powder (see page 40), for garnish

Heat a non-stick griddle pan over high heat and grill the kabocha for 1 — 2 minutes on each side until lightly charred and cooked through.

Place a wok over medium — high heat, add the butter and oil then quickly toss through the garlic, mushrooms and spring onion. Cook for 1 — 2 minutes, add the soy sauce and toss to combine.

To assemble the ramen, quickly and evenly divide the drained noodles between two bowls and pour over the hot shio broth. Add the stir-fried mushrooms, vegetable gyoza, nori, kabocha and corn. Dot the miso butter bombs on the corn and sprinkle over the sesame seeds. Garnish with a little umami mushroom powder.

GROUND CHICKEN WITH SPICY
BEAN PASTE SHIO RAMEN

SERVES 2

1 tablespoon peanut oil

300 g (10½ oz) minced (ground) chicken

¼ teaspoon ground white pepper

1 tablespoon mirin

2 teaspoons caster (superfine) sugar

1 tablespoon soy sauce

1 tablespoon spicy chilli bean paste (la doubanjiang), or to taste (see notes)

2 teaspoons finely grated ginger

1 spring onion (scallion), thinly sliced

2 portions thin Ramen Noodles (see page 20), cooked al dente and drained

800 ml (27 fl oz) Shio Broth (see page 17), simmering

120 g (4½ oz) silken tofu, cubed

Black Mayu (see page 40), for drizzling

bean sprouts, for garnish

dried chilli threads, for garnish (see notes)

Heat the oil in a wok over medium — high heat. Add the chicken and stir-fry for 2 — 3 minutes, breaking up the meat with a wooden spoon. Add the pepper, mirin, sugar, soy sauce, spicy chilli bean paste and ginger, and cook for a further 1 — 2 minutes. Toss through the spring onion and set aside.

To assemble the ramen, quickly and evenly divide the drained noodles between two bowls and pour over the hot shio broth. Add the stir-fried chicken mixture and tofu. Drizzle over a little black mayu and garnish with bean sprouts and chilli threads.

NOTES

La doubanjiang can be purchased from most Asian supermarkets. Dried chilli threads are also known as Korean chilli threads, silgochu or chilli strings. They can be purchased from most Asian supermarkets.

CURRY BOWLS

SEAFOOD LAKSA

SERVES 2

1 tablespoon peanut oil

6 raw prawns (shrimp), shelled with tails left intact, deveined

150 g (5½ oz) squid tubes, cleaned and cut into 1 cm (½ in) thick slices

80 g (2¾ oz/⅓ cup) laksa paste (see page 22)

juice of 1 lime, plus lime wedges, to serve

2 kaffir lime leaves

2 teaspoons grated palm sugar (jaggery)

300 ml (10 fl oz) coconut milk

300 ml (10 fl oz) Simple Chicken Stock (see page 17)

300 ml (10 fl oz) Dashi Stock (see page 19)

1 tablespoon fish sauce

2 portions thin Ramen Noodles (see page 20), cooked al dente and drained

4 tofu puffs, halved

1 baby bok choy, halved and blanched

coriander (cilantro) leaves, to serve

mint leaves, to serve

fried shallots, to serve

bean sprouts, to serve

Heat the 1 tablespoon oil in a wok over high heat, add the prawns and squid and stir-fry for 1 — 2 minutes, until the squid is opaque and the prawns are just cooked. Remove from the pan and set aside.

Reduce the heat to medium, add the laksa paste and cook, stirring, for 1 — 2 minutes until fragrant.

Add the lime juice, lime leaves, sugar, coconut milk and stocks and bring to a rapid simmer. Add the fish sauce, taste, and add more if desired, then cook for 1 — 2 minutes.

Divide the drained noodles between two bowls and top with the prawns and squid. Pour over the laksa broth and top with the tofu puffs and blanched bok choy. Sprinkle over a few coriander and mint leaves, some fried shallots and bean sprouts. Serve with lime wedges for squeezing over.

HIYASHI CHUKA

COLD RAMEN SALAD

SERVES 2

2 portions thin Ramen Noodles (see page 20), cooked al dente, then chilled in iced water and well drained

100 g (3½ oz) store-bought barbecued chicken, shredded

2 Ajitsuke Tamago (see page 26), halved

6 cherry tomatoes, halved

2 radishes, thinly sliced

1 small carrot, julienned

1 spring onion (scallion), thinly sliced

½ small Persian cucumber, julienned

pickled ginger (*beni shoga*), to serve

snow pea (mangetout) tendrils, for garnish

black sesame seeds, for garnish

Japanese Quick Pickles (see page 38), to serve

Pickled Shiitake Mushrooms (see page 37), to serve

DRESSING

80 ml (2½ fl oz/⅓ cup) Dashi Stock (see page 19)

60 ml (2 fl oz/¼ cup) soy sauce

2 tablespoons mirin

1 tablespoon rice wine vinegar

1 tablespoon sake

1 tablespoon toasted sesame oil

½ teaspoon chilli oil

1½ teaspoons caster (superfine) sugar

½ teaspoon freshly grated ginger

½ teaspoon toasted sesame seeds

Whisk the dressing ingredients together in a small bowl.

Divide the chilled noodles between two bowls and top with the chicken, ajitsuke tamago, cherry tomato, radish, carrot, spring onion and cucumber. Pour over the dressing and top with a little pickled ginger. Garnish with the snow pea tendrils and sesame seeds, and serve with the pickles on the side.

JAPANESE CURRY

SERVES 2

2 tablespoons peanut oil

400 g (14 oz) stewing beef, cut into 5 cm (2 in) cubes

sea salt and ground white pepper

30 g (1 oz) butter

½ onion, finely diced

2 garlic cloves, finely grated

2 teaspoons freshly grated ginger

1½ tablespoons Japanese curry powder

2 tablespoons plain (all purpose) flour

300 ml (10 fl oz) Simple Chicken Stock (see page 17)

300 ml (10 fl oz) Dashi Stock (see page 19)

1 tablespoon soy sauce

1 teaspoon brown sugar

1 teaspoon rice wine

½ green apple, peeled and grated

100 g (3½ oz) carrots, cut rangiri-style (see note)

300 g (10½ oz) potatoes, quartered

TO SERVE

2 portions thick Ramen Noodles (see page 20), cooked al dente and drained

2 Ajitsuke Tamago (see page 26), halved

thinly sliced spring onions (scallions)

sesame chilli oil

fermented bamboo shoots (menma)

Heat the oil in a frying pan over medium — high heat. Season the beef with salt and pepper, then sear for 5 — 7 minutes until browned on all sides. Remove from the pan and set aside.

Reduce the heat to medium — low and melt the butter. Add the onion and sauté for 4 minutes, then add the garlic and ginger and sauté for a further 2 minutes or until the onion is soft. Add the curry powder and flour and cook, stirring, for 1 — 2 minutes. Gradually whisk in the stocks, until smooth. Add the soy sauce, sugar and rice wine, and stir to combine.

Add the seared beef, apple, carrot and potato and simmer for 1½ — 2 hours or until tender.

Divide the noodles between two bowls. Spoon over the curry and top with the ajitsuke tamago and spring onion. Drizzle over a little sesame chilli oil and serve with fermented bamboo shoots on the side.

NOTE

Rangiri is a style of cutting long vegetables (carrots, daikon etc) for stews, where you cut the vegetable on the diagonal while rotating a quarter turn between cuts. This allows a maximum surface area to absorb the flavour.

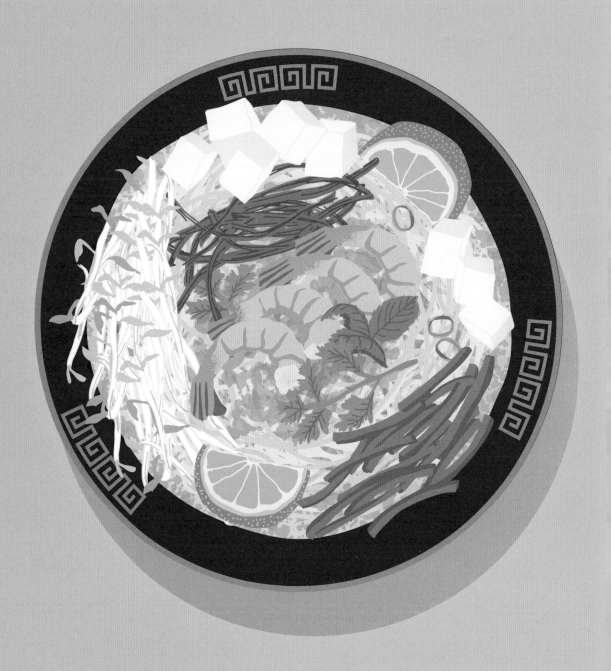

THAI GREEN CURRY WITH PRAWNS AND TOFU

SERVES 2

1 tablespoon coconut oil

80 g (2¾ oz/⅓ cup) Thai green curry paste (see page 23)

400 ml (13½ fl oz) coconut cream

125 ml (4 fl oz/½ cup) Simple Chicken Stock (see page 17)

125 ml (4 fl oz/½ cup) Dashi Stock (see page 19)

2 kaffir lime leaves

1 — 2 tablespoons fish sauce, to taste

1 tablespoon grated palm sugar

2 tablespoons lime juice

70 g (2½ oz) carrot, julienned

8 raw prawns (shrimp), shelled with tails left intact, deveined

60 g (2 oz) firm tofu, cut into cubes

8 snow peas (mangetout), julienned

small handful Thai basil leaves

small handful coriander (cilantro) leaves

2 portions Ramen Noodles (see page 20), cooked al dente and drained

bean sprouts, for garnish

lime wedges, to serve

Heat the coconut oil in a wok over medium — high heat and add the Thai green curry paste. Fry for 1 — 2 minutes until fragrant. Add the coconut cream, stocks, lime leaves, fish sauce, sugar and lime juice and stir to combine. Taste, and add more fish sauce if desired.

Bring to the boil, then reduce the heat and add the carrot. Simmer for 1 minute, then add the prawns and tofu and cook for a further 1 minute. Finally, add the snow peas, Thai basil and coriander leaves and cook for 40 — 60 seconds.

Divide the drained noodles between two bowls, ladle over the curry and garnish with bean sprouts. Serve with lime wedges on the side for squeezing over.

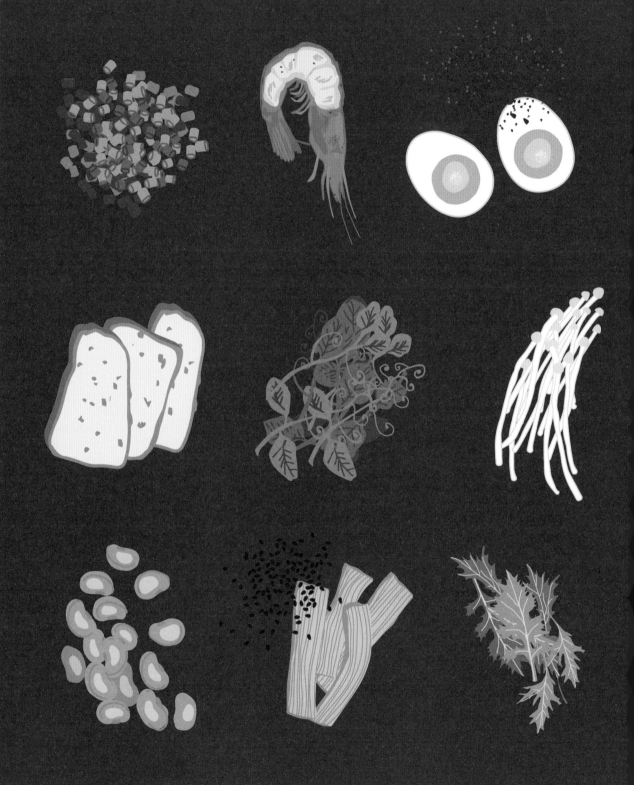

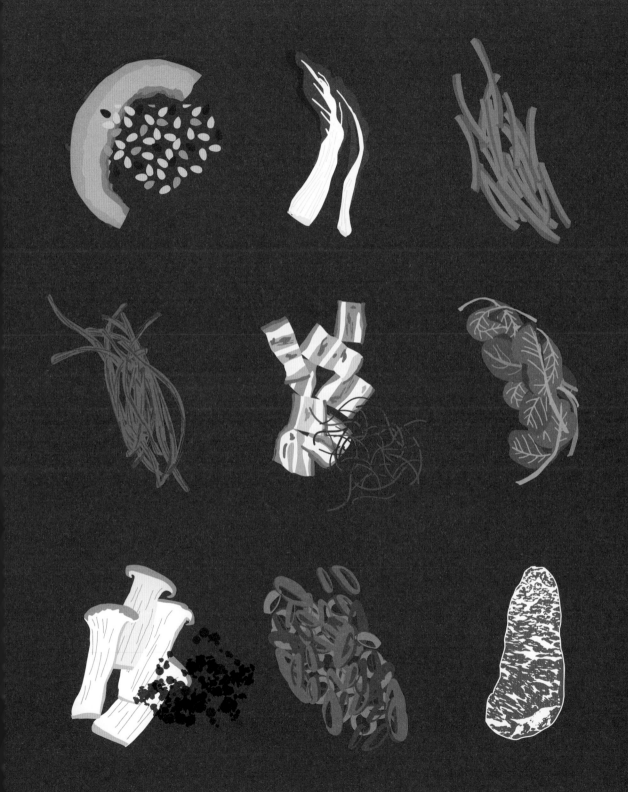

INDEX BY INGREDIENT

INDEX BY BASE

Smith Street Books

Published in 2017 by Smith Street Books
Melbourne | Australia
smithstreetbooks.com

ISBN: 978-1-9254-1851-4

CIP data is available from the National
Library of Australia

Publisher: Paul McNally
Recipes and text: Deborah Kaloper
Editor: Lucy Heaver
Project manager: Aisling Coughlan
Design & art direction: Michelle Mackintosh
Design layout: Kirby Jones
Illustrator: Alice Oehr

Printed & bound in China by C&C Offset
Printing Co., Ltd.

Book 38
10 9 8 7 6 5 4 3 2 1

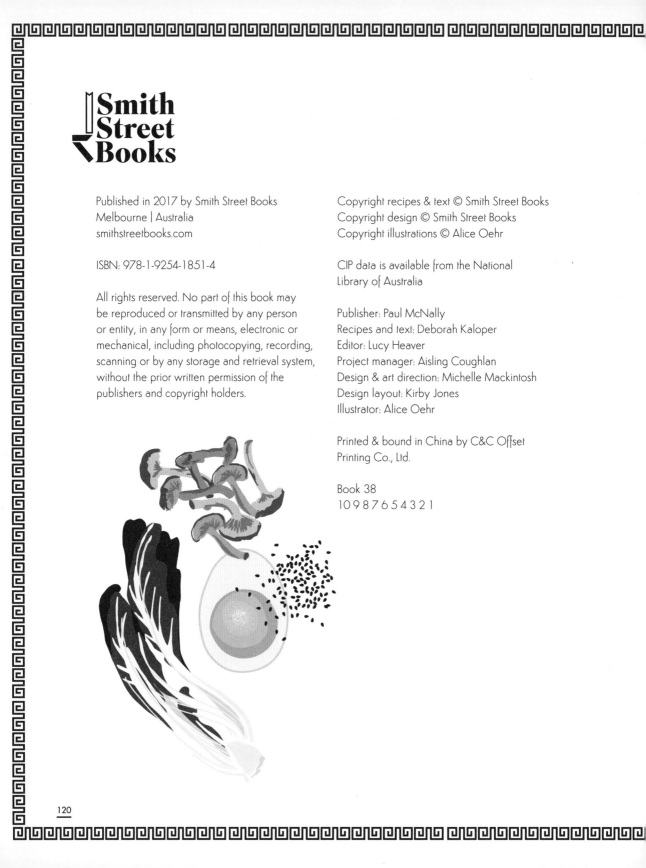

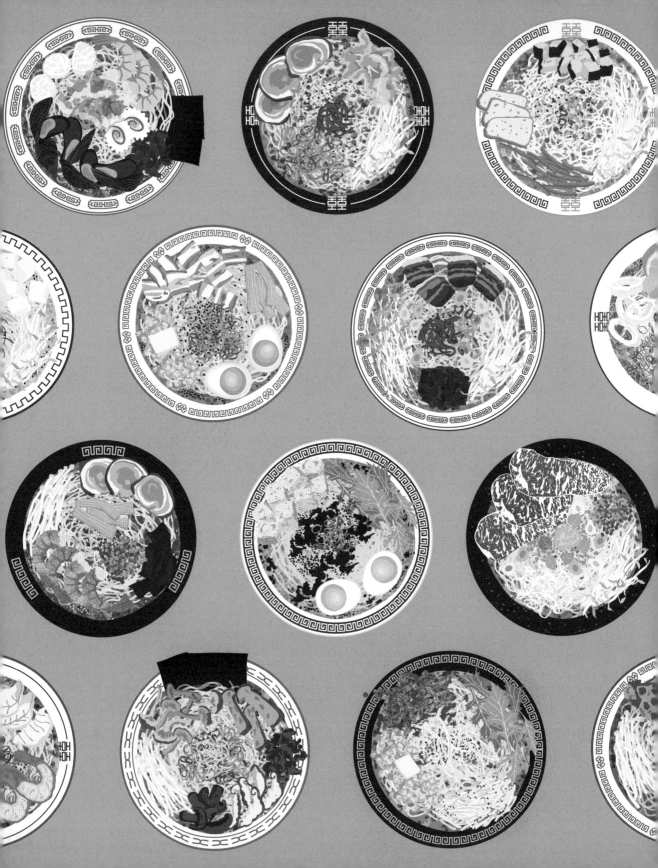